C-4365　　CAREER EXAMINATION SERIES

This is your
PASSBOOK for...

Water Utility Operator

Test Preparation Study Guide
Questions & Answers

COPYRIGHT NOTICE

This book is SOLELY intended for, is sold ONLY to, and its use is RESTRICTED to individual, bona fide applicants or candidates who qualify by virtue of having seriously filed applications for appropriate license, certificate, professional and/or promotional advancement, higher school matriculation, scholarship, or other legitimate requirements of education and/or governmental authorities.

This book is NOT intended for use, class instruction, tutoring, training, duplication, copying, reprinting, excerption, or adaptation, etc., by:

1) Other publishers
2) Proprietors and/or Instructors of "Coaching" and/or Preparatory Courses
3) Personnel and/or Training Divisions of commercial, industrial, and governmental organizations
4) Schools, colleges, or universities and/or their departments and staffs, including teachers and other personnel
5) Testing Agencies or Bureaus
6) Study groups which seek by the purchase of a single volume to copy and/or duplicate and/or adapt this material for use by the group as a whole without having purchased individual volumes for each of the members of the group
7) Et al.

Such persons would be in violation of appropriate Federal and State statutes.

PROVISION OF LICENSING AGREEMENTS – Recognized educational, commercial, industrial, and governmental institutions and organizations, and others legitimately engaged in educational pursuits, including training, testing, and measurement activities, may address request for a licensing agreement to the copyright owners, who will determine whether, and under what conditions, including fees and charges, the materials in this book may be used them. In other words, a licensing facility exists for the legitimate use of the material in this book on other than an individual basis. However, it is asseverated and affirmed here that the material in this book CANNOT be used without the receipt of the express permission of such a licensing agreement from the Publishers. Inquiries re licensing should be addressed to the company, attention rights and permissions department.

All rights reserved, including the right of reproduction in whole or in part, in any form or by any means, electronic or mechanical, including photocopying, recording, or by any information storage and retrieval system, without permission in writing from the Publisher.

Copyright © 2025 by
National Learning Corporation

212 Michael Drive, Syosset, NY 11791
(516) 921-8888 • www.passbooks.com
E-mail: info@passbooks.com

PASSBOOK® SERIES

THE *PASSBOOK® SERIES* has been created to prepare applicants and candidates for the ultimate academic battlefield – the examination room.

At some time in our lives, each and every one of us may be required to take an examination – for validation, matriculation, admission, qualification, registration, certification, or licensure.

Based on the assumption that every applicant or candidate has met the basic formal educational standards, has taken the required number of courses, and read the necessary texts, the *PASSBOOK® SERIES* furnishes the one special preparation which may assure passing with confidence, instead of failing with insecurity. Examination questions – together with answers – are furnished as the basic vehicle for study so that the mysteries of the examination and its compounding difficulties may be eliminated or diminished by a sure method.

This book is meant to help you pass your examination provided that you qualify and are serious in your objective.

The entire field is reviewed through the huge store of content information which is succinctly presented through a provocative and challenging approach – the question-and-answer method.

A climate of success is established by furnishing the correct answers at the end of each test.

You soon learn to recognize types of questions, forms of questions, and patterns of questioning. You may even begin to anticipate expected outcomes.

You perceive that many questions are repeated or adapted so that you can gain acute insights, which may enable you to score many sure points.

You learn how to confront new questions, or types of questions, and to attack them confidently and work out the correct answers.

You note objectives and emphases, and recognize pitfalls and dangers, so that you may make positive educational adjustments.

Moreover, you are kept fully informed in relation to new concepts, methods, practices, and directions in the field.

You discover that you are actually taking the examination all the time: you are preparing for the examination by "taking" an examination, not by reading extraneous and/or supererogatory textbooks.

In short, this PASSBOOK®, used directedly, should be an important factor in helping you to pass your test.

WATER UTILITY OPERATOR

A Water Utility Operator inspects, operates, and maintains electric water pumping plants, reservoirs, wells and related water facilities; patrols reservoirs to locate hazardous or potentially hazardous conditions; and monitors the operation.

SCOPE OF THE EXAMINATION
The written test will be of the multiple choices and will test in the above related areas.

HOW TO TAKE A TEST

I. YOU MUST PASS AN EXAMINATION

A. WHAT EVERY CANDIDATE SHOULD KNOW

Examination applicants often ask us for help in preparing for the written test. What can I study in advance? What kinds of questions will be asked? How will the test be given? How will the papers be graded?

As an applicant for a civil service examination, you may be wondering about some of these things. Our purpose here is to suggest effective methods of advance study and to describe civil service examinations.

Your chances for success on this examination can be increased if you know how to prepare. Those "pre-examination jitters" can be reduced if you know what to expect. You can even experience an adventure in good citizenship if you know why civil service exams are given.

B. WHY ARE CIVIL SERVICE EXAMINATIONS GIVEN?

Civil service examinations are important to you in two ways. As a citizen, you want public jobs filled by employees who know how to do their work. As a job seeker, you want a fair chance to compete for that job on an equal footing with other candidates. The best-known means of accomplishing this two-fold goal is the competitive examination.

Exams are widely publicized throughout the nation. They may be administered for jobs in federal, state, city, municipal, town or village governments or agencies.

Any citizen may apply, with some limitations, such as the age or residence of applicants. Your experience and education may be reviewed to see whether you meet the requirements for the particular examination. When these requirements exist, they are reasonable and applied consistently to all applicants. Thus, a competitive examination may cause you some uneasiness now, but it is your privilege and safeguard.

C. HOW ARE CIVIL SERVICE EXAMS DEVELOPED?

Examinations are carefully written by trained technicians who are specialists in the field known as "psychological measurement," in consultation with recognized authorities in the field of work that the test will cover. These experts recommend the subject matter areas or skills to be tested; only those knowledges or skills important to your success on the job are included. The most reliable books and source materials available are used as references. Together, the experts and technicians judge the difficulty level of the questions.

Test technicians know how to phrase questions so that the problem is clearly stated. Their ethics do not permit "trick" or "catch" questions. Questions may have been tried out on sample groups, or subjected to statistical analysis, to determine their usefulness.

Written tests are often used in combination with performance tests, ratings of training and experience, and oral interviews. All of these measures combine to form the best-known means of finding the right person for the right job.

II. HOW TO PASS THE WRITTEN TEST

A. NATURE OF THE EXAMINATION

To prepare intelligently for civil service examinations, you should know how they differ from school examinations you have taken. In school you were assigned certain definite pages to read or subjects to cover. The examination questions were quite detailed and usually emphasized memory. Civil service exams, on the other hand, try to discover your present ability to perform the duties of a position, plus your potentiality to learn these duties. In other words, a civil service exam attempts to predict how successful you will be. Questions cover such a broad area that they cannot be as minute and detailed as school exam questions.

In the public service similar kinds of work, or positions, are grouped together in one "class." This process is known as *position-classification*. All the positions in a class are paid according to the salary range for that class. One class title covers all of these positions, and they are all tested by the same examination.

B. FOUR BASIC STEPS

1) Study the announcement

How, then, can you know what subjects to study? Our best answer is: "Learn as much as possible about the class of positions for which you've applied." The exam will test the knowledge, skills and abilities needed to do the work.

Your most valuable source of information about the position you want is the official exam announcement. This announcement lists the training and experience qualifications. Check these standards and apply only if you come reasonably close to meeting them.

The brief description of the position in the examination announcement offers some clues to the subjects which will be tested. Think about the job itself. Review the duties in your mind. Can you perform them, or are there some in which you are rusty? Fill in the blank spots in your preparation.

Many jurisdictions preview the written test in the exam announcement by including a section called "Knowledge and Abilities Required," "Scope of the Examination," or some similar heading. Here you will find out specifically what fields will be tested.

2) Review your own background

Once you learn in general what the position is all about, and what you need to know to do the work, ask yourself which subjects you already know fairly well and which need improvement. You may wonder whether to concentrate on improving your strong areas or on building some background in your fields of weakness. When the announcement has specified "some knowledge" or "considerable knowledge," or has used adjectives like "beginning principles of…" or "advanced … methods," you can get a clue as to the number and difficulty of questions to be asked in any given field. More questions, and hence broader coverage, would be included for those subjects which are more important in the work. Now weigh your strengths and weaknesses against the job requirements and prepare accordingly.

3) Determine the level of the position

Another way to tell how intensively you should prepare is to understand the level of the job for which you are applying. Is it the entering level? In other words, is this the position in which beginners in a field of work are hired? Or is it an intermediate or advanced level? Sometimes this is indicated by such words as "Junior" or "Senior" in the class title. Other jurisdictions use Roman numerals to designate the level – Clerk I, Clerk II, for example. The word "Supervisor" sometimes appears in the title. If the level is not indicated by the title, check the description of duties. Will you be working under very close supervision, or will you have responsibility for independent decisions in this work?

4) Choose appropriate study materials

Now that you know the subjects to be examined and the relative amount of each subject to be covered, you can choose suitable study materials. For beginning level jobs, or even advanced ones, if you have a pronounced weakness in some aspect of your training, read a modern, standard textbook in that field. Be sure it is up to date and has general coverage. Such books are normally available at your library, and the librarian will be glad to help you locate one. For entry-level positions, questions of appropriate difficulty are chosen – neither highly advanced questions, nor those too simple. Such questions require careful thought but not advanced training.

If the position for which you are applying is technical or advanced, you will read more advanced, specialized material. If you are already familiar with the basic principles of your field, elementary textbooks would waste your time. Concentrate on advanced textbooks and technical periodicals. Think through the concepts and review difficult problems in your field.

These are all general sources. You can get more ideas on your own initiative, following these leads. For example, training manuals and publications of the government agency which employs workers in your field can be useful, particularly for technical and professional positions. A letter or visit to the government department involved may result in more specific study suggestions, and certainly will provide you with a more definite idea of the exact nature of the position you are seeking.

III. KINDS OF TESTS

Tests are used for purposes other than measuring knowledge and ability to perform specified duties. For some positions, it is equally important to test ability to make adjustments to new situations or to profit from training. In others, basic mental abilities not dependent on information are essential. Questions which test these things may not appear as pertinent to the duties of the position as those which test for knowledge and information. Yet they are often highly important parts of a fair examination. For very general questions, it is almost impossible to help you direct your study efforts. What we can do is to point out some of the more common of these general abilities needed in public service positions and describe some typical questions.

1) General information

Broad, general information has been found useful for predicting job success in some kinds of work. This is tested in a variety of ways, from vocabulary lists to questions about current events. Basic background in some field of work, such as sociology or economics, may be sampled in a group of questions. Often these are principles which have become familiar to most persons through exposure rather than through formal training. It is difficult to advise you how to study for these questions; being alert to the world around you is our best suggestion.

2) Verbal ability

An example of an ability needed in many positions is verbal or language ability. Verbal ability is, in brief, the ability to use and understand words. Vocabulary and grammar tests are typical measures of this ability. Reading comprehension or paragraph interpretation questions are common in many kinds of civil service tests. You are given a paragraph of written material and asked to find its central meaning.

3) Numerical ability

Number skills can be tested by the familiar arithmetic problem, by checking paired lists of numbers to see which are alike and which are different, or by interpreting charts and graphs. In the latter test, a graph may be printed in the test booklet which you are asked to use as the basis for answering questions.

4) Observation

A popular test for law-enforcement positions is the observation test. A picture is shown to you for several minutes, then taken away. Questions about the picture test your ability to observe both details and larger elements.

5) Following directions

In many positions in the public service, the employee must be able to carry out written instructions dependably and accurately. You may be given a chart with several columns, each column listing a variety of information. The questions require you to carry out directions involving the information given in the chart.

6) Skills and aptitudes

Performance tests effectively measure some manual skills and aptitudes. When the skill is one in which you are trained, such as typing or shorthand, you can practice. These tests are often very much like those given in business school or high school courses. For many of the other skills and aptitudes, however, no short-time preparation can be made. Skills and abilities natural to you or that you have developed throughout your lifetime are being tested.

Many of the general questions just described provide all the data needed to answer the questions and ask you to use your reasoning ability to find the answers. Your best preparation for these tests, as well as for tests of facts and ideas, is to be at your physical and mental best. You, no doubt, have your own methods of getting into an exam-taking mood and keeping "in shape." The next section lists some ideas on this subject.

IV. KINDS OF QUESTIONS

Only rarely is the "essay" question, which you answer in narrative form, used in civil service tests. Civil service tests are usually of the short-answer type. Full instructions for answering these questions will be given to you at the examination. But in case this is your first experience with short-answer questions and separate answer sheets, here is what you need to know:

1) Multiple-choice Questions

Most popular of the short-answer questions is the "multiple choice" or "best answer" question. It can be used, for example, to test for factual knowledge, ability to solve problems or judgment in meeting situations found at work.

A multiple-choice question is normally one of three types—
- It can begin with an incomplete statement followed by several possible endings. You are to find the one ending which *best* completes the statement, although some of the others may not be entirely wrong.
- It can also be a complete statement in the form of a question which is answered by choosing one of the statements listed.

- It can be in the form of a problem – again you select the best answer.

Here is an example of a multiple-choice question with a discussion which should give you some clues as to the method for choosing the right answer:

When an employee has a complaint about his assignment, the action which will *best* help him overcome his difficulty is to
- A. discuss his difficulty with his coworkers
- B. take the problem to the head of the organization
- C. take the problem to the person who gave him the assignment
- D. say nothing to anyone about his complaint

In answering this question, you should study each of the choices to find which is best. Consider choice "A" – Certainly an employee may discuss his complaint with fellow employees, but no change or improvement can result, and the complaint remains unresolved. Choice "B" is a poor choice since the head of the organization probably does not know what assignment you have been given, and taking your problem to him is known as "going over the head" of the supervisor. The supervisor, or person who made the assignment, is the person who can clarify it or correct any injustice. Choice "C" is, therefore, correct. To say nothing, as in choice "D," is unwise. Supervisors have and interest in knowing the problems employees are facing, and the employee is seeking a solution to his problem.

2) True/False Questions

The "true/false" or "right/wrong" form of question is sometimes used. Here a complete statement is given. Your job is to decide whether the statement is right or wrong.

SAMPLE: A roaming cell-phone call to a nearby city costs less than a non-roaming call to a distant city.

This statement is wrong, or false, since roaming calls are more expensive.

This is not a complete list of all possible question forms, although most of the others are variations of these common types. You will always get complete directions for answering questions. Be sure you understand *how* to mark your answers – ask questions until you do.

V. RECORDING YOUR ANSWERS

Computer terminals are used more and more today for many different kinds of exams.

For an examination with very few applicants, you may be told to record your answers in the test booklet itself. Separate answer sheets are much more common. If this separate answer sheet is to be scored by machine – and this is often the case – it is highly important that you mark your answers correctly in order to get credit.

An electronic scoring machine is often used in civil service offices because of the speed with which papers can be scored. Machine-scored answer sheets must be marked with a pencil, which will be given to you. This pencil has a high graphite content which responds to the electronic scoring machine. As a matter of fact, stray dots may register as answers, so do not let your pencil rest on the answer sheet while you are pondering the correct answer. Also, if your pencil lead breaks or is otherwise defective, ask for another.

Since the answer sheet will be dropped in a slot in the scoring machine, be careful not to bend the corners or get the paper crumpled.

The answer sheet normally has five vertical columns of numbers, with 30 numbers to a column. These numbers correspond to the question numbers in your test booklet. After each number, going across the page are four or five pairs of dotted lines. These short dotted lines have small letters or numbers above them. The first two pairs may also have a "T" or "F" above the letters. This indicates that the first two pairs only are to be used if the questions are of the true-false type. If the questions are multiple choice, disregard the "T" and "F" and pay attention only to the small letters or numbers.

Answer your questions in the manner of the sample that follows:

32. The largest city in the United States is
    A. Washington, D.C.
    B. New York City
    C. Chicago
    D. Detroit
    E. San Francisco

1) Choose the answer you think is best. (New York City is the largest, so "B" is correct.)
2) Find the row of dotted lines numbered the same as the question you are answering. (Find row number 32)
3) Find the pair of dotted lines corresponding to the answer. (Find the pair of lines under the mark "B.")
4) Make a solid black mark between the dotted lines.

VI. BEFORE THE TEST

Common sense will help you find procedures to follow to get ready for an examination. Too many of us, however, overlook these sensible measures. Indeed, nervousness and fatigue have been found to be the most serious reasons why applicants fail to do their best on civil service tests. Here is a list of reminders:

- Begin your preparation early – Don't wait until the last minute to go scurrying around for books and materials or to find out what the position is all about.
- Prepare continuously – An hour a night for a week is better than an all-night cram session. This has been definitely established. What is more, a night a week for a month will return better dividends than crowding your study into a shorter period of time.
- Locate the place of the exam – You have been sent a notice telling you when and where to report for the examination. If the location is in a different town or otherwise unfamiliar to you, it would be well to inquire the best route and learn something about the building.
- Relax the night before the test – Allow your mind to rest. Do not study at all that night. Plan some mild recreation or diversion; then go to bed early and get a good night's sleep.
- Get up early enough to make a leisurely trip to the place for the test – This way unforeseen events, traffic snarls, unfamiliar buildings, etc. will not upset you.
- Dress comfortably – A written test is not a fashion show. You will be known by number and not by name, so wear something comfortable.

- Leave excess paraphernalia at home – Shopping bags and odd bundles will get in your way. You need bring only the items mentioned in the official notice you received; usually everything you need is provided. Do not bring reference books to the exam. They will only confuse those last minutes and be taken away from you when in the test room.
- Arrive somewhat ahead of time – If because of transportation schedules you must get there very early, bring a newspaper or magazine to take your mind off yourself while waiting.
- Locate the examination room – When you have found the proper room, you will be directed to the seat or part of the room where you will sit. Sometimes you are given a sheet of instructions to read while you are waiting. Do not fill out any forms until you are told to do so; just read them and be prepared.
- Relax and prepare to listen to the instructions
- If you have any physical problem that may keep you from doing your best, be sure to tell the test administrator. If you are sick or in poor health, you really cannot do your best on the exam. You can come back and take the test some other time.

VII. AT THE TEST

The day of the test is here and you have the test booklet in your hand. The temptation to get going is very strong. Caution! There is more to success than knowing the right answers. You must know how to identify your papers and understand variations in the type of short-answer question used in this particular examination. Follow these suggestions for maximum results from your efforts:

1) Cooperate with the monitor

The test administrator has a duty to create a situation in which you can be as much at ease as possible. He will give instructions, tell you when to begin, check to see that you are marking your answer sheet correctly, and so on. He is not there to guard you, although he will see that your competitors do not take unfair advantage. He wants to help you do your best.

2) Listen to all instructions

Don't jump the gun! Wait until you understand all directions. In most civil service tests you get more time than you need to answer the questions. So don't be in a hurry. Read each word of instructions until you clearly understand the meaning. Study the examples, listen to all announcements and follow directions. Ask questions if you do not understand what to do.

3) Identify your papers

Civil service exams are usually identified by number only. You will be assigned a number; you must not put your name on your test papers. Be sure to copy your number correctly. Since more than one exam may be given, copy your exact examination title.

4) Plan your time

Unless you are told that a test is a "speed" or "rate of work" test, speed itself is usually not important. Time enough to answer all the questions will be provided, but this does not mean that you have all day. An overall time limit has been set. Divide the total time (in minutes) by the number of questions to determine the approximate time you have for each question.

5) Do not linger over difficult questions

If you come across a difficult question, mark it with a paper clip (useful to have along) and come back to it when you have been through the booklet. One caution if you do this – be sure to skip a number on your answer sheet as well. Check often to be sure that you have not lost your place and that you are marking in the row numbered the same as the question you are answering.

6) Read the questions

Be sure you know what the question asks! Many capable people are unsuccessful because they failed to *read* the questions correctly.

7) Answer all questions

Unless you have been instructed that a penalty will be deducted for incorrect answers, it is better to guess than to omit a question.

8) Speed tests

It is often better NOT to guess on speed tests. It has been found that on timed tests people are tempted to spend the last few seconds before time is called in marking answers at random – without even reading them – in the hope of picking up a few extra points. To discourage this practice, the instructions may warn you that your score will be "corrected" for guessing. That is, a penalty will be applied. The incorrect answers will be deducted from the correct ones, or some other penalty formula will be used.

9) Review your answers

If you finish before time is called, go back to the questions you guessed or omitted to give them further thought. Review other answers if you have time.

10) Return your test materials

If you are ready to leave before others have finished or time is called, take ALL your materials to the monitor and leave quietly. Never take any test material with you. The monitor can discover whose papers are not complete, and taking a test booklet may be grounds for disqualification.

VIII. EXAMINATION TECHNIQUES

1) Read the general instructions carefully. These are usually printed on the first page of the exam booklet. As a rule, these instructions refer to the timing of the examination; the fact that you should not start work until the signal and must stop work at a signal, etc. If there are any *special* instructions, such as a choice of questions to be answered, make sure that you note this instruction carefully.

2) When you are ready to start work on the examination, that is as soon as the signal has been given, read the instructions to each question booklet, underline any key words or phrases, such as *least, best, outline, describe* and the like. In this way you will tend to answer as requested rather than discover on reviewing your paper that you *listed without describing*, that you selected the *worst* choice rather than the *best* choice, etc.

3) If the examination is of the objective or multiple-choice type – that is, each question will also give a series of possible answers: A, B, C or D, and you are called upon to select the best answer and write the letter next to that answer on your answer paper – it is advisable to start answering each question in turn. There may be anywhere from 50 to 100 such questions in the three or four hours allotted and you can see how much time would be taken if you read through all the questions before beginning to answer any. Furthermore, if you come across a question or group of questions which you know would be difficult to answer, it would undoubtedly affect your handling of all the other questions.

4) If the examination is of the essay type and contains but a few questions, it is a moot point as to whether you should read all the questions before starting to answer any one. Of course, if you are given a choice – say five out of seven and the like – then it is essential to read all the questions so you can eliminate the two that are most difficult. If, however, you are asked to answer all the questions, there may be danger in trying to answer the easiest one first because you may find that you will spend too much time on it. The best technique is to answer the first question, then proceed to the second, etc.

5) Time your answers. Before the exam begins, write down the time it started, then add the time allowed for the examination and write down the time it must be completed, then divide the time available somewhat as follows:
    - If 3-1/2 hours are allowed, that would be 210 minutes. If you have 80 objective-type questions, that would be an average of 2-1/2 minutes per question. Allow yourself no more than 2 minutes per question, or a total of 160 minutes, which will permit about 50 minutes to review.
    - If for the time allotment of 210 minutes there are 7 essay questions to answer, that would average about 30 minutes a question. Give yourself only 25 minutes per question so that you have about 35 minutes to review.

6) The most important instruction is to *read each question* and make sure you know what is wanted. The second most important instruction is to *time yourself properly* so that you answer every question. The third most important instruction is to *answer every question*. Guess if you have to but include something for each question. Remember that you will receive no credit for a blank and will probably receive some credit if you write something in answer to an essay question. If you guess a letter – say "B" for a multiple-choice question – you may have guessed right. If you leave a blank as an answer to a multiple-choice question, the examiners may respect your feelings but it will not add a point to your score. Some exams may penalize you for wrong answers, so in such cases *only*, you may not want to guess unless you have some basis for your answer.

7) Suggestions
    a. Objective-type questions
        1. Examine the question booklet for proper sequence of pages and questions
        2. Read all instructions carefully
        3. Skip any question which seems too difficult; return to it after all other questions have been answered
        4. Apportion your time properly; do not spend too much time on any single question or group of questions

       5. Note and underline key words – *all, most, fewest, least, best, worst, same, opposite,* etc.
       6. Pay particular attention to negatives
       7. Note unusual option, e.g., unduly long, short, complex, different or similar in content to the body of the question
       8. Observe the use of "hedging" words – *probably, may, most likely,* etc.
       9. Make sure that your answer is put next to the same number as the question
      10. Do not second-guess unless you have good reason to believe the second answer is definitely more correct
      11. Cross out original answer if you decide another answer is more accurate; do not erase until you are ready to hand your paper in
      12. Answer all questions; guess unless instructed otherwise
      13. Leave time for review

  b. Essay questions
       1. Read each question carefully
       2. Determine exactly what is wanted. Underline key words or phrases.
       3. Decide on outline or paragraph answer
       4. Include many different points and elements unless asked to develop any one or two points or elements
       5. Show impartiality by giving pros and cons unless directed to select one side only
       6. Make and write down any assumptions you find necessary to answer the questions
       7. Watch your English, grammar, punctuation and choice of words
       8. Time your answers; don't crowd material

8) Answering the essay question

Most essay questions can be answered by framing the specific response around several key words or ideas. Here are a few such key words or ideas:

M's: manpower, materials, methods, money, management
P's: purpose, program, policy, plan, procedure, practice, problems, pitfalls, personnel, public relations

  a. Six basic steps in handling problems:
       1. Preliminary plan and background development
       2. Collect information, data and facts
       3. Analyze and interpret information, data and facts
       4. Analyze and develop solutions as well as make recommendations
       5. Prepare report and sell recommendations
       6. Install recommendations and follow up effectiveness

  b. Pitfalls to avoid
       1. *Taking things for granted* – A statement of the situation does not necessarily imply that each of the elements is necessarily true; for example, a complaint may be invalid and biased so that all that can be taken for granted is that a complaint has been registered

2. *Considering only one side of a situation* – Wherever possible, indicate several alternatives and then point out the reasons you selected the best one
3. *Failing to indicate follow up* – Whenever your answer indicates action on your part, make certain that you will take proper follow-up action to see how successful your recommendations, procedures or actions turn out to be
4. *Taking too long in answering any single question* – Remember to time your answers properly

IX. AFTER THE TEST

Scoring procedures differ in detail among civil service jurisdictions although the general principles are the same. Whether the papers are hand-scored or graded by machine we have described, they are nearly always graded by number. That is, the person who marks the paper knows only the number – never the name – of the applicant. Not until all the papers have been graded will they be matched with names. If other tests, such as training and experience or oral interview ratings have been given, scores will be combined. Different parts of the examination usually have different weights. For example, the written test might count 60 percent of the final grade, and a rating of training and experience 40 percent. In many jurisdictions, veterans will have a certain number of points added to their grades.

After the final grade has been determined, the names are placed in grade order and an eligible list is established. There are various methods for resolving ties between those who get the same final grade – probably the most common is to place first the name of the person whose application was received first. Job offers are made from the eligible list in the order the names appear on it. You will be notified of your grade and your rank as soon as all these computations have been made. This will be done as rapidly as possible.

People who are found to meet the requirements in the announcement are called "eligibles." Their names are put on a list of eligible candidates. An eligible's chances of getting a job depend on how high he stands on this list and how fast agencies are filling jobs from the list.

When a job is to be filled from a list of eligibles, the agency asks for the names of people on the list of eligibles for that job. When the civil service commission receives this request, it sends to the agency the names of the three people highest on this list. Or, if the job to be filled has specialized requirements, the office sends the agency the names of the top three persons who meet these requirements from the general list.

The appointing officer makes a choice from among the three people whose names were sent to him. If the selected person accepts the appointment, the names of the others are put back on the list to be considered for future openings.

That is the rule in hiring from all kinds of eligible lists, whether they are for typist, carpenter, chemist, or something else. For every vacancy, the appointing officer has his choice of any one of the top three eligibles on the list. This explains why the person whose name is on top of the list sometimes does not get an appointment when some of the persons lower on the list do. If the appointing officer chooses the second or third eligible, the No. 1 eligible does not get a job at once, but stays on the list until he is appointed or the list is terminated.

X. HOW TO PASS THE INTERVIEW TEST

The examination for which you applied requires an oral interview test. You have already taken the written test and you are now being called for the interview test – the final part of the formal examination.

You may think that it is not possible to prepare for an interview test and that there are no procedures to follow during an interview. Our purpose is to point out some things you can do in advance that will help you and some good rules to follow and pitfalls to avoid while you are being interviewed.

What is an interview supposed to test?

The written examination is designed to test the technical knowledge and competence of the candidate; the oral is designed to evaluate intangible qualities, not readily measured otherwise, and to establish a list showing the relative fitness of each candidate – as measured against his competitors – for the position sought. Scoring is not on the basis of "right" and "wrong," but on a sliding scale of values ranging from "not passable" to "outstanding." As a matter of fact, it is possible to achieve a relatively low score without a single "incorrect" answer because of evident weakness in the qualities being measured.

Occasionally, an examination may consist entirely of an oral test – either an individual or a group oral. In such cases, information is sought concerning the technical knowledges and abilities of the candidate, since there has been no written examination for this purpose. More commonly, however, an oral test is used to supplement a written examination.

Who conducts interviews?

The composition of oral boards varies among different jurisdictions. In nearly all, a representative of the personnel department serves as chairman. One of the members of the board may be a representative of the department in which the candidate would work. In some cases, "outside experts" are used, and, frequently, a businessman or some other representative of the general public is asked to serve. Labor and management or other special groups may be represented. The aim is to secure the services of experts in the appropriate field.

However the board is composed, it is a good idea (and not at all improper or unethical) to ascertain in advance of the interview who the members are and what groups they represent. When you are introduced to them, you will have some idea of their backgrounds and interests, and at least you will not stutter and stammer over their names.

What should be done before the interview?

While knowledge about the board members is useful and takes some of the surprise element out of the interview, there is other preparation which is more substantive. It *is* possible to prepare for an oral interview – in several ways:

1) Keep a copy of your application and review it carefully before the interview

This may be the only document before the oral board, and the starting point of the interview. Know what education and experience you have listed there, and the sequence and dates of all of it. Sometimes the board will ask you to review the highlights of your experience for them; you should not have to hem and haw doing it.

2) Study the class specification and the examination announcement

Usually, the oral board has one or both of these to guide them. The qualities, characteristics or knowledges required by the position sought are stated in these documents. They offer valuable clues as to the nature of the oral interview. For example, if the job involves supervisory responsibilities, the announcement will usually indicate that knowledge of modern supervisory methods and the qualifications of the candidate as a supervisor will be tested. If so, you can expect such questions, frequently in the form of a hypothetical situation which you are expected to solve. NEVER go into an oral without knowledge of the duties and responsibilities of the job you seek.

3) Think through each qualification required

Try to visualize the kind of questions you would ask if you were a board member. How well could you answer them? Try especially to appraise your own knowledge and background in each area, *measured against the job sought*, and identify any areas in which you are weak. Be critical and realistic – do not flatter yourself.

4) Do some general reading in areas in which you feel you may be weak

For example, if the job involves supervision and your past experience has NOT, some general reading in supervisory methods and practices, particularly in the field of human relations, might be useful. Do NOT study agency procedures or detailed manuals. The oral board will be testing your understanding and capacity, not your memory.

5) Get a good night's sleep and watch your general health and mental attitude

You will want a clear head at the interview. Take care of a cold or any other minor ailment, and of course, no hangovers.

What should be done on the day of the interview?

Now comes the day of the interview itself. Give yourself plenty of time to get there. Plan to arrive somewhat ahead of the scheduled time, particularly if your appointment is in the fore part of the day. If a previous candidate fails to appear, the board might be ready for you a bit early. By early afternoon an oral board is almost invariably behind schedule if there are many candidates, and you may have to wait. Take along a book or magazine to read, or your application to review, but leave any extraneous material in the waiting room when you go in for your interview. In any event, relax and compose yourself.

The matter of dress is important. The board is forming impressions about you – from your experience, your manners, your attitude, and your appearance. Give your personal appearance careful attention. Dress your best, but not your flashiest. Choose conservative, appropriate clothing, and be sure it is immaculate. This is a business interview, and your appearance should indicate that you regard it as such. Besides, being well groomed and properly dressed will help boost your confidence.

Sooner or later, someone will call your name and escort you into the interview room. *This is it.* From here on you are on your own. It is too late for any more preparation. But remember, you asked for this opportunity to prove your fitness, and you are here because your request was granted.

What happens when you go in?

The usual sequence of events will be as follows: The clerk (who is often the board stenographer) will introduce you to the chairman of the oral board, who will introduce you to the other members of the board. Acknowledge the introductions before you sit down. Do not be surprised if you find a microphone facing you or a stenotypist sitting by. Oral interviews are usually recorded in the event of an appeal or other review.

Usually the chairman of the board will open the interview by reviewing the highlights of your education and work experience from your application – primarily for the benefit of the other members of the board, as well as to get the material into the record. Do not interrupt or comment unless there is an error or significant misinterpretation; if that is the case, do not hesitate. But do not quibble about insignificant matters. Also, he will usually ask you some question about your education, experience or your present job – partly to get you to start talking and to establish the interviewing "rapport." He may start the actual questioning, or turn it over to one of the other members. Frequently, each member undertakes the questioning on a particular area, one in which he is perhaps most competent, so you can expect each member to participate in the examination. Because time is limited, you may also expect some rather abrupt switches in the direction the questioning takes, so do not be upset by it. Normally, a board member will not pursue a single line of questioning unless he discovers a particular strength or weakness.

After each member has participated, the chairman will usually ask whether any member has any further questions, then will ask you if you have anything you wish to add. Unless you are expecting this question, it may floor you. Worse, it may start you off on an extended, extemporaneous speech. The board is not usually seeking more information. The question is principally to offer you a last opportunity to present further qualifications or to indicate that you have nothing to add. So, if you feel that a significant qualification or characteristic has been overlooked, it is proper to point it out in a sentence or so. Do not compliment the board on the thoroughness of their examination – they have been sketchy, and you know it. If you wish, merely say, "No thank you, I have nothing further to add." This is a point where you can "talk yourself out" of a good impression or fail to present an important bit of information. Remember, *you close the interview yourself*.

The chairman will then say, "That is all, Mr. _____, thank you." Do not be startled; the interview is over, and quicker than you think. Thank him, gather your belongings and take your leave. Save your sigh of relief for the other side of the door.

How to put your best foot forward

Throughout this entire process, you may feel that the board individually and collectively is trying to pierce your defenses, seek out your hidden weaknesses and embarrass and confuse you. Actually, this is not true. They are obliged to make an appraisal of your qualifications for the job you are seeking, and they want to see you in your best light. Remember, they must interview all candidates and a non-cooperative candidate may become a failure in spite of their best efforts to bring out his qualifications. Here are 15 suggestions that will help you:

1) Be natural – Keep your attitude confident, not cocky

If you are not confident that you can do the job, do not expect the board to be. Do not apologize for your weaknesses, try to bring out your strong points. The board is interested in a positive, not negative, presentation. Cockiness will antagonize any board member and make him wonder if you are covering up a weakness by a false show of strength.

2) Get comfortable, but don't lounge or sprawl

Sit erectly but not stiffly. A careless posture may lead the board to conclude that you are careless in other things, or at least that you are not impressed by the importance of the occasion. Either conclusion is natural, even if incorrect. Do not fuss with your clothing, a pencil or an ashtray. Your hands may occasionally be useful to emphasize a point; do not let them become a point of distraction.

3) Do not wisecrack or make small talk

This is a serious situation, and your attitude should show that you consider it as such. Further, the time of the board is limited – they do not want to waste it, and neither should you.

4) Do not exaggerate your experience or abilities

In the first place, from information in the application or other interviews and sources, the board may know more about you than you think. Secondly, you probably will not get away with it. An experienced board is rather adept at spotting such a situation, so do not take the chance.

5) If you know a board member, do not make a point of it, yet do not hide it

Certainly you are not fooling him, and probably not the other members of the board. Do not try to take advantage of your acquaintanceship – it will probably do you little good.

6) Do not dominate the interview

Let the board do that. They will give you the clues – do not assume that you have to do all the talking. Realize that the board has a number of questions to ask you, and do not try to take up all the interview time by showing off your extensive knowledge of the answer to the first one.

7) Be attentive

You only have 20 minutes or so, and you should keep your attention at its sharpest throughout. When a member is addressing a problem or question to you, give him your undivided attention. Address your reply principally to him, but do not exclude the other board members.

8) Do not interrupt

A board member may be stating a problem for you to analyze. He will ask you a question when the time comes. Let him state the problem, and wait for the question.

9) Make sure you understand the question

Do not try to answer until you are sure what the question is. If it is not clear, restate it in your own words or ask the board member to clarify it for you. However, do not haggle about minor elements.

10) Reply promptly but not hastily

A common entry on oral board rating sheets is "candidate responded readily," or "candidate hesitated in replies." Respond as promptly and quickly as you can, but do not jump to a hasty, ill-considered answer.

11) Do not be peremptory in your answers

A brief answer is proper – but do not fire your answer back. That is a losing game from your point of view. The board member can probably ask questions much faster than you can answer them.

12) Do not try to create the answer you think the board member wants

He is interested in what kind of mind you have and how it works – not in playing games. Furthermore, he can usually spot this practice and will actually grade you down on it.

13) Do not switch sides in your reply merely to agree with a board member

Frequently, a member will take a contrary position merely to draw you out and to see if you are willing and able to defend your point of view. Do not start a debate, yet do not surrender a good position. If a position is worth taking, it is worth defending.

14) Do not be afraid to admit an error in judgment if you are shown to be wrong

The board knows that you are forced to reply without any opportunity for careful consideration. Your answer may be demonstrably wrong. If so, admit it and get on with the interview.

15) Do not dwell at length on your present job

The opening question may relate to your present assignment. Answer the question but do not go into an extended discussion. You are being examined for a *new* job, not your present one. As a matter of fact, try to phrase ALL your answers in terms of the job for which you are being examined.

Basis of Rating

Probably you will forget most of these "do's" and "don'ts" when you walk into the oral interview room. Even remembering them all will not ensure you a passing grade. Perhaps you did not have the qualifications in the first place. But remembering them will help you to put your best foot forward, without treading on the toes of the board members.

Rumor and popular opinion to the contrary notwithstanding, an oral board wants you to make the best appearance possible. They know you are under pressure – but they also want to see how you respond to it as a guide to what your reaction would be under the pressures of the job you seek. They will be influenced by the degree of poise you display, the personal traits you show and the manner in which you respond.

ABOUT THIS BOOK

This book contains tests divided into Examination Sections. Go through each test, answering every question in the margin. We have also attached a sample answer sheet at the back of the book that can be removed and used. At the end of each test look at the answer key and check your answers. On the ones you got wrong, look at the right answer choice and learn. Do not fill in the answers first. Do not memorize the questions and answers, but understand the answer and principles involved. On your test, the questions will likely be different from the samples. Questions are changed and new ones added. If you understand these past questions you should have success with any changes that arise. Tests may consist of several types of questions. We have additional books on each subject should more study be advisable or necessary for you. Finally, the more you study, the better prepared you will be. This book is intended to be the last thing you study before you walk into the examination room. Prior study of relevant texts is also recommended. NLC publishes some of these in our Fundamental Series. Knowledge and good sense are important factors in passing your exam. Good luck also helps. So now study this Passbook, absorb the material contained within and take that knowledge into the examination. Then do your best to pass that exam.

EXAMINATION SECTION

EXAMINATION SECTION
TEST 1

DIRECTIONS: Each question or incomplete statement is followed by several suggested answers or completions. Select the one that BEST answers the question or completes the statement. *PRINT THE LETTER OF THE CORRECT ANSWER IN THE SPACE AT THE RIGHT.*

1. When filling an empty aqueduct, the valve should be opened

    A. slowly to prevent damage to the aqueduct
    B. rapidly to fill the line as soon as possible
    C. slowly to prevent rapid lowering of the reservoir level
    D. rapidly so that there are no air locks

2. The BEST way of detecting the location of a suspected chlorine leak is by placing a _____ near the suspected leak.

    A. rag, which has been dipped in a strong ammonia water,
    B. match
    C. piece of litmus paper
    D. flow meter

3. The term *run-off* refers to the

    A. amount a valve must be turned in order to open it fully
    B. length of time an electric motor continues to turn after the current is shut off
    C. amount of rainfall which flows from the ground surface into the streams and reservoirs
    D. distance the water falls from the intake gate to the turbine

4. Algae in reservoirs may be killed by using

    A. zeolite   B. copper sulphate
    C. sodium chloride   D. calcium chloride

5. The one of the following types of valves that USUALLY operates without manual control is a(n) _____ valve.

    A. check   B. globe   C. gate   D. angle

6. Rate of flow of water through a water treatment plant is USUALLY referred to in terms of

    A. c.f.s.   B. c.f.m.   C. r.p.m.   D. m.g.d.

7. In order to make it easier to operate a large valve or gate, pressures on both sides of the valve or gate are balanced by

    A. using weights on each side of the valve or gate
    B. opening a smaller by-pass valve
    C. partially shutting down the water in the upstream line
    D. opening the downstream valve very slowly

8. Leaves are removed from the water entering the treatment plant or aqueduct by

    A. skimming   B. coagulating   C. draining   D. screening

9. Odors, due to gases in the water, are removed by

   A. surging B. sluicing C. aerating D. clarifying

10. Chlorine residual refers to the

    A. amount of chlorine that must be added to the water
    B. amount of chlorine that remains in the water after a given period
    C. method of adding the chlorine to the water
    D. method of protecting personnel using chlorine from the effects of the chlorine

11. One of the processes that takes place in an Imhoff tank is

    A. oxidation B. flocculation C. digestion D. coagulation

12. As used in a sewage disposal plant, *effluent* refers to the

    A. basic treatment process of sewage
    B. time it takes for complete treatment of sewage
    C. type of control the plant uses for treatment
    D. final liquid coming out of the treatment process

13. A grit chamber operates on the basis that

    A. grit will settle out of slow-moving water
    B. grit will float and can be removed by skimming the surface
    C. increasing the rate of flow of water will leave the grit behind
    D. spraying water into the air will cause the heavier grit to separate from the water

14. The purpose of sedimentation in any sewage treatment process is to

    A. aerate the sewage
    B. increase the chlorine content of the sewage
    C. remove suspended matter from the sewage
    D. kill the bacteria in the sewage

15. The final treatment for sludge before it is disposed of is

    A. drying B. adding chlorine
    C. mixing D. washing

16. The amount of sewage applied to a filter bed is GENERALLY controlled by a

    A. sluice gate B. flow meter
    C. dosing siphon D. regulating valve

17. Methane gas which results from the sewage treatment process is MOST frequently

    A. vented to the outside air to prevent injury to plant personnel
    B. used as a fuel in the plant
    C. combined with other gases to render it harmless
    D. burned in the open air

18. The filtering material in a *filter bed* at a sewage treatment plant is USUALLY

    A. activated charcoal B. sand
    C. alum D. ammonium chloride

19. Cleaning sewer lines is USUALLY done by the use of a

　　A. catch basin　　　　　　　　B. flushometer
　　C. sewer rod　　　　　　　　　D. center line

20. One of the ways of locating a leak in a water line is by using a

　　A. manometer　　　　　　　　B. sounding rod
　　C. poling board　　　　　　　D. diffusor

21. MOST sewer pipes are made of

　　A. cast iron　　　　　　　　　B. agricultural tile
　　C. brass　　　　　　　　　　　D. copper

22. One of the materials generally used in caulking joints in bell and spigot pipe is

　　A. tar　　　B. litharge　　　C. red lead　　　D. oakum

23. Water pipe must be laid at least two feet below the ground surface MAINLY to

　　A. prevent freezing
　　B. discourage malicious tampering
　　C. reduce the pressure required to make the water flow
　　D. eliminate possibility of damage to roads in case of water main break

24. When soldering copper gutters, the flux that is GENERALLY used is

　　A. sal ammoniac　　　　　　　B. resin
　　C. killed muriatic acid　　　　D. calcium chloride

25. A good concrete mix for use in the foundations of a small building is

　　A. 1:2:5　　　B. 5:2:1　　　C. 2:5:1　　　D. 1:5:2

26. When painting steel, red lead is used MAINLY as a

　　A. primer coat so final coat will adhere better
　　B. primer coat to protect the steel from rusting
　　C. finish coat to protect the steel from the action of the sun and water
　　D. second coat to bind the primer and finish coats

27. Studs in frame buildings are USUALLY

　　A. 1" x 4"　　　B. 1" x 6"　　　C. 2" x 4"　　　D. 2" x 6"

28. A cement mortar used in brickwork is USUALLY made more workable by adding

　　A. phosphate　　　B. lime　　　C. calcium　　　D. grout

Questions 29-32.

　　DIRECTIONS:　The following four questions numbered 29 to 32, inclusive, are to be answered in accordance with the rules of the department of water supply, gas and electricity.

29. The term *water course* refers to 29.____

    A. aqueducts only
    B. pipe lines only
    C. natural or artificial streams only
    D. all of the above

30. Where a swimming pool discharges upon or into the ground and the water is not treated, 30.____
    the minimum distance between such discharge and a stream MUST be at least _____
    feet.

    A. 50   B. 100   C. 250   D. 450

31. According to the above rules, clothes may 31.____

    A. be washed in a spring, if the spring does not feed directly into a reservoir
    B. be washed in a spring if the place where this is being done is at least one mile from a reservoir
    C. be washed in a spring provided a chlorinated soap is used
    D. not be washed in a spring

32. Industrial wastes may 32.____

    A. be discharged into a stream provided the stream does not feed directly into a reservoir
    B. be discharged into a stream, provided the point of discharge is at least one mile from a reservoir
    C. be discharged into a stream if the wastes are purified in an approved manner
    D. not be discharged into a stream

33. One method of determining the height of the water in a stream feeding into a reservoir is 33.____
    by means of a

    A. venturi meter   B. flow meter
    C. hook gage   D. strain gage

34. When digging a deep trench, the sides are USUALLY prevented from caving in by using 34.____

    A. shoulders   B. blocking   C. pins   D. sheathing

35. The FIRST precaution a worker should take before entering a sewer manhole is to 35.____

    A. put on hard-toed shoes
    B. put on safety goggles
    C. check that the next manhole upstream is not obstructed
    D. test the air in the manhole

36. Assume that a fuse blows upon connecting a light load to the circuit. You replace it with 36.____
    the same size fuse, and again the fuse blows.
    The BEST thing to do in this case is to

    A. connect a wire across the fuse so it cannot blow under such a light load
    B. replace the fuse with one having a higher rating
    C. check the wiring of the circuit
    D. place two fuses in series to prevent blowing

37. Of the following material, the one that is BEST for fill as a subgrade for a road is

    A. sand
    B. silt
    C. clay
    D. a mixture of sand, silt, and clay

38. When dealing with leaking chlorine, it is IMPORTANT to remember that chlorine is

    A. highly flammable
    B. made safe by spraying water on it
    C. not corrosive
    D. heavier than air

39. Cast iron pipe is MOST frequently cut with a(n)

    A. hack saw
    B. diamond point chisel
    C. burning torch
    D. abrasive wheel

40. Water hammer in a pipe line is BEST reduced by installing

    A. a pressure regulator
    B. an air chamber
    C. smaller pipes and valves
    D. larger pipes and valves

KEY (CORRECT ANSWERS)

1. A	11. C	21. A	31. D
2. A	12. D	22. D	32. D
3. C	13. A	23. A	33. C
4. B	14. C	24. C	34. D
5. A	15. A	25. A	35. D
6. D	16. C	26. B	36. C
7. B	17. B	27. C	37. D
8. D	18. B	28. B	38. D
9. C	19. C	29. D	39. B
10. B	20. B	30. B	40. B

TEST 2

DIRECTIONS: Each question or incomplete statement is followed by several suggested answers or completions. Select the one that BEST answers the question or completes the statement. *PRINT THE LETTER OF THE CORRECT ANSWER IN SPACE AT THE RIGHT.*

1. When used in conjunction with a centrifugal pump, a foot valve

    A. equalizes the pressure on both sides of the pump
    B. regulates the amount of water flowing through the pump
    C. prevents water in the pump from flowing back down the suction line
    D. adjusts the speed of the pump to the amount of water to be pumped

2. Grounding an electric motor is

    A. *good* practice because the motor will operate better
    B. *poor* practice because the motor will not operate as well
    C. *good* practice because it protects against shock hazards
    D. *poor* practice because it increases shock hazards

3. The one of the following wrenches that should NOT be used to turn a nut is a _____ wrench.

    A. monkey   B. box   C. stillson   D. socket

4. A drill is GENERALLY removed from the chuck of a portable electric drill by using a

    A. drift pin   B. wedge
    C. centerpunch   D. key

5. The finished surface of a dirt road is MOST frequently maintained with a

    A. blade grader   B. bulldozer
    C. dragline   D. carryall

6. Frequent stalling of a truck engine is MOST probably due to a

    A. weak battery   B. low battery water level
    C. leaking oil filter   D. dirty carburetor

7. If the reading of the oil pressure gage on a gasoline motor should suddenly drop to zero, the FIRST thing the operator should do is to

    A. check the filter
    B. inspect the oil lines
    C. tighten the oil pan bolts
    D. stop the motor

8. A tractor is to be stored for two months. In order to keep it in BEST condition, it should be

    A. drained of all fuel and oil
    B. lubricated every week
    C. started up periodically and run until warm
    D. steam cleaned and all water drained from the radiator

9. Trees suffering from transplanting shock are quickly helped by

A. deep watering B. foliage feeding
C. root feeding D. vitamin treatments

10. For MOST rapid healing, trees should be pruned during

    A. November, December, and January
    B. February, March, and April
    C. May, June, and July
    D. August, September, and October

11. The blades of a lawn mower should be set so that the blades

    A. firmly touch the bed knife
    B. barely touch the bed knife
    C. clear the bed knife by 1/16 inch
    D. clear the bed knife by 1/8 inch

12. The MAIN reason for mulching is to

    A. fertilize the soil
    B. prevent erosion
    C. protect plants from the cold
    D. kill insects

13. A compost heap would MOST likely include

    A. lawn clippings B. sand
    C. stumps of trees D. gravel

14. Of the following statements with regard to *seeding,* the one that is CORRECT is:

    A. Seeds should be sown on a windy day
    B. The ground should be watered heavily after seeding
    C. Seeding should be done primarily on a bright and sunny day
    D. It is not necessary to carefully apportion the amount of seeds sown

15. Organic matter is often added to soil to better condition it for growing plants. Of the following, the item that is NOT organic matter is

    A. lime B. peat C. manure D. leaf mold

16. Of the following, the BEST way to store coniferous seedlings which cannot be planted for a few days is to

    A. unwrap them and put them in a dark, dry location
    B. place them flat on the ground in a sunny location so they can get plenty of light and air
    C. place them in a trench dug in the earth and cover the root ends with soil
    D. make sure the ball is not loosened and keep in a hothouse

17. Transplanting of seedlings is BEST done in early

    A. spring B. summer C. autumn D. winter

18. After planting privet hedges, they are frequently cut back to within a few inches of the ground.
    This is USUALLY done to

    A. remove dead parts of the hedge
    B. insure dense growth from the ground up
    C. speed up root development
    D. reduce the possibility of insect damage while the hedge is taking root

18.____

19. *Heaving* of pavements in wintertime is USUALLY caused by the

    A. difference of expansion of pavement and subgrade
    B. freezing of water in subgrade
    C. loss of bond between pavement and subgrade
    D. brittleness of pavement

19.____

20. Erosion of side slopes caused by the action of water is GREATEST when the soil is

    A. silt   B. clay   C. hardpan   D. silty-clay

20.____

21. The MAIN reason for making a crown in a road pavement is to

    A. reduce the amount of paving material necessary
    B. make it easier for cars to go around a curve
    C. drain surface water
    D. increase the strength of the pavement where it is most needed

21.____

22. The MAIN reason for paving ditches at the side of a road is to

    A. prevent damage from cars
    B. permit the ditch to carry more water
    C. prevent erosion of the soil in the ditch
    D. block water from getting under the pavement

22.____

23. Assume that vitrified clay tile pipe, with open joints, is being used as the underdrain for a roadway.
    This pipe should be laid

    A. directly on the bottom of the trench
    B. on a bed of clay
    C. on a bed of peat
    D. on a bed of gravel

23.____

24. A macadam road is one in which the base is GENERALLY made of

    A. asphalt   B. broken stone
    C. concrete   D. stabilized soil

24.____

25. To loosen compacted rocky earth road surfaces, the BEST piece of equipment to use is a

    A. disc harrow   B. drag line   C. bulldozer   D. scarifier

25.____

26. Oiling of an earth road is BEST done

    A. in the winter before the snow falls
    B. when you expect much rain

26.____

C. in the spring during dry weather
D. immediately after snow is cleared from the road

27. Cracks in concrete roads are BEST repaired by filling them with   27.____

   A. tar   B. grout
   C. mineral filler   D. sand

28. When repairing patches in old asphalt pavements, the edges of the patch should FIRST   28.____
    be painted with

   A. the same material used for the patch
   B. kerosene
   C. asphalt cement
   D. asphalt binder

29. The sum of 3 1/4, 5 1/8, 2 1/2, and 3 3/8 is   29.____

   A. 14   B. 14 1/8   C. 14 1/4   D. 14 3/8

30. Assume that it takes 6 men 8 days to do a particular job.   30.____
    If you have only 4 men available to do this job and they all work at the same speed,
    then the number of days it would take to complete the job would be

   A. 11   B. 12   C. 13   D. 14

31. The city aims to supply *potable* water. As used in this sentence, the word *potable* means   31.____
    MOST NEARLY

   A. clear   B. drinkable   C. fresh   D. adequate

32. Water, after being purified, should not be turbid. As used in this sentence, the word *turbid*   32.____
    means MOST NEARLY

   A. cloudy   B. warm   C. infected D. hard

33. The flow of water is *impeded* by the silt in the bottom of the stream.   33.____
    As used in this sentence, the word *impeded* means MOST NEARLY

   A. dammed   B. hindered   C. helped   D. dirtied

Questions 34-35.

DIRECTIONS: Questions 34 and 35 are based on the following paragraph.

Repeated burning of the same area should be avoided. Burning should not be done on impervious, shallow, unstable, or highly erodible soils, or on steep slopes - especially in areas subject to heavy rains or rapid snowmelt. When existing vegetation is likely to be killed or seriously weakened by the fire, measures should be taken to assure prompt revegetation of the burned area. Burns should be limited to relatively small proportions of a watershed unit so that the stream channels will be able to carry any increased flows with a minimum of damage.

34. According to the above paragraph, planned burning should be limited to small areas of the watershed because

    A. the fire can be better controlled
    B. existing vegetation will be less likely to be killed
    C. plants will grow quicker in small areas
    D. there will be less likelihood of damaging floods

35. According to the above paragraph, burning usually should be done on soils that

    A. readily absorb moisture
    B. have been burnt before
    C. exist as a thin layer over rock
    D. can be flooded by nearby streams

36. If a foreman does not understand the instructions that are given to him by the district engineer, the BEST thing to do is to

    A. work out the solution to the problem himself
    B. do the job in the way he thinks is best
    C. get one of the other foremen to do the job
    D. ask that the instructions be repeated and clarified

37. The BEST foreman is the one who

    A. can work as fast as the fastest man in the crew
    B. is the most skilled mechanic
    C. can get the most work out of the men
    D. is the strongest man

38. Complimenting a man for good work is

    A. *good* practice since it will give the man an incentive to continue working well
    B. *poor* practice because the other men will become jealous
    C. *good* practice because in the future the foreman will not have to supervise this man
    D. *poor* practice since the man should work well without needing compliments

39. In dealing with his men, it is MOST important that a foreman be

    A. a disciplinarian   B. stern
    C. fair   D. chummy with his men

40. When issuing a violation to a member of the public, it is MOST important that a foreman be

    A. aloof and refuse to discuss the violation
    B. stern, and warn the person to correct the violation immediately
    C. courteous and explain what must be done to correct the violation
    D. friendly and volunteer assistance to correct the violation

KEY (CORRECT ANSWERS)

1.	C	11.	B	21.	C	31.	B
2.	C	12.	C	22.	C	32.	A
3.	C	13.	A	23.	D	33.	B
4.	D	14.	B	24.	B	34.	D
5.	A	15.	A	25.	D	35.	A
6.	D	16.	C	26.	C	36.	D
7.	D	17.	A	27.	A	37.	C
8.	C	18.	B	28.	C	38.	A
9.	B	19.	B	29.	C	39.	C
10.	B	20.	A	30.	B	40.	C

EXAMINATION SECTION
TEST 1

DIRECTIONS: Each question or incomplete statement is followed by several suggested answers or completions. Select the one that *BEST* answers the question or completes the statement. *PRINT THE LETTER OF THE CORRECT ANSWER IN THE SPACE AT THE RIGHT.*

1. When 60,987 is added to 27,835, the result is
   A. 80,712   B. 80,822   C. 87,712   D. 88,822

2. The sum of 693 + 787 + 946 + 355 + 731 is
   A. 3,512   B. 3,502   C. 3,412   D. 3,402

3. When 2,586 is subtracted from 3,003, the result is
   A. 417   B. 527   C. 1,417   D. 1,527

4. When 1.32 is subtracted from 52.6, the result is
   A. 3.94   B. 5.128   C. 39.4   D. 51.28

5. When 56 is multiplied by 438, the result is
   A. 840   B. 4,818   C. 24,528   D. 48,180

6. When 8.7 is multiplied by .34, the result is, most nearly,
   A. 2.9   B. 3.0   C. 29.5   D. 29.6

7. When 1/2 is divided by 2/3, the result is
   A. 1/3   B. 3/4   C. 1 1/3   D. 3

8. When 8,340 is divided by 38, the result is, most nearly
   A. 210   B. 218   C. 219   D. 220

Questions 9-11.

DIRECTIONS: Questions 9 to 11 inclusive are to be answered *SOLELY* on the basis of the information given below.

Assume that a certain water treatment plant has consumed quantities of chemicals E and F over a five-week period, as indicated in the following table:

Time Period	Number of 100-pound sacks consumed	
	Chemical E	Chemical F
Week 1	5	4
Week 2	7	5
Week 3	6	5
Week 4	8	6
Week 5	6	4

9. The *total* number of pounds of chemical E consumed at the end of the first three weeks is   9.____

   A. 180   B. 320   C. 1,400   D. 1,800

10. According to the table, the week in which the *most* chemicals were consumed was   10.____

    A. week 2   B. week 3   C. week 4   D. week 5

11. According to the table, the *average* number of sacks of chemical F consumed over the first four weeks was   11.____

    A. 4   B. 5   C. 6   D. 7

12. Of the following actions, the *best* one to take FIRST after smoke is seen coming from an electric control device is to   12.____

    A. shut off the power to it
    B. call the main office for advice
    C. look for a wiring diagram
    D. throw water on it

13. Of the following items, the one which would LEAST likely be included on a memorandum is the   13.____

    A. home address of the writer of the memorandum
    B. name of the writer of the memorandum
    C. subject of the memorandum
    D. names or titles of the person who will receive the memorandum

14. When testing joints for leaks in pipe lines containing natural gas, it is BEST to use   14.____

    A. water in the lines under pressure
    B. a lighted candle
    C. an aquastat
    D. soapy water

Questions 15-17.

DIRECTIONS: Questions 15 to 17 inclusive are to be answered SOLELY on the basis of the information given below.

Assume that at various hours of a typical day the amounts of chlorine residual in parts per million (ppm) at a certain water treatment plant are as shown in the following graph:

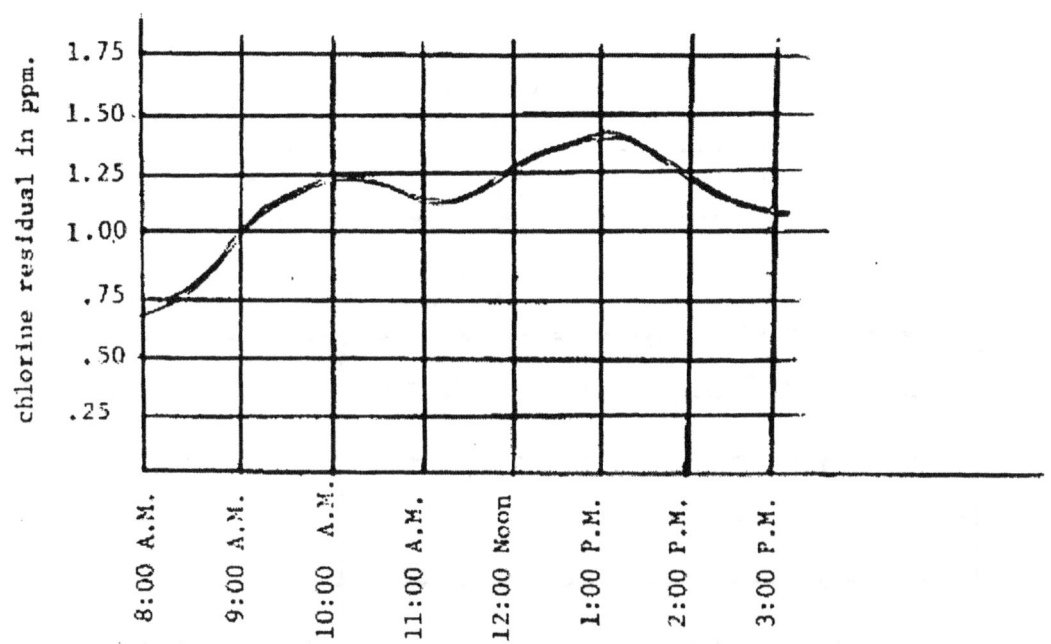

15. According to the graph, the chlorine residual measured in ppm at 9:00 A.M. was, most nearly,

    A. .70   B. .75   C. 1.00   D. 1.25

16. The maximum chlorine residual between 8:00 A.M. and 3:00 P.M. was, most nearly,

    A. .68 ppm   B. 1.10 ppm   C. 1.25 ppm   D. 1.37 ppm

17. According to the graph, between the hour of 12:00 Noon and 1:00 P.M., the chlorine residual was

    A. always increasing
    B. always decreasing
    C. increasing, then decreasing
    D. decreasing, then increasing

18. Of the following statements concerning the use and care of wooden ladders, the *one* which is *TRUE* is that

    A. a light oil should be applied to the rungs to preserve the wood
    B. each rung should be sharply struck with a metal hammer to test its soundness before using it
    C. ladders should be stored in a warm damp area to prevent the wood from getting brittle
    D. tops of ordinary stepladders should not be used as steps

19. It is *poor* practice to use gasoline to clean metal parts that are coated with grease *PRIMARILY* because gasoline

    A. contains lead which is harmful to the user
    B. is a poor solvent for grease
    C. corrodes metal
    D. vapors ignite easily

Questions 20-21.

DIRECTIONS: Questions 20 and 21 are to be answered SOLELY on the basis of the information given in the tables below.

	Inventory of 100 pound bags on hand as of 1-1	
	Chemical X	16 1/2
	Chemical Y	12

Date	Chemical	Number of 100 pound bags used	Number of 100 pound bags received
1-5	X	8 1/2	
1-9	X	3 1/2	
1-9	Y	5	
1-14	X		8
1-18	Y	2 1/2	
1-23	X	3	
1-27	Y	4 1/2	
1-30	X		2
1-31	X	1	

	Inventory of 100 pound bags on hand as of 1-31	
	Chemical X	
	Chemical Y	

J. Doe 2-2
Operator

20. According to the information given in the table, the number of 100-pound bags of chemical Y *on hand* as of 1-31 is

    A. 0   B. 1/2   C. 1   D. 1 1/2

21. According to the information in the table, the *total* number of pounds of chemical X consumed in the month was, most nearly,

    A. 500   B. 1,600   C. 1,800   D. 2,800

Questions 22-27.

DIRECTIONS: Questions 22 to 27 inclusive are to be answered SOLELY on the basis of the paragraph below.

FIRST AID INSTRUCTIONS

The main purpose of first aid is to put the injured person in the best possible position until medical help arrives. This includes the performance of emergency treatment for the purpose of saving a life if a doctor is not present. When a person is hurt, a crowd usually gathers around the victim. If nobody uses his head, the injured person fails to get the care he needs. You must stay calm and, most important, it is your duty to take charge at an accident. The first thing for you to do is to see, as best you can, what is wrong with the injured person. Leave the victim where he is until the nature and extent of his injury are determined. If he is unconscious he should not be moved except to lay him flat on his back if he is in some other position. Loosen the clothing of any seriously hurt person and make him as comfortable as possible. Medical help should be called as soon as possible. You should remain with the injured person and send someone else to call the doctor. You should try to make sure that the one who calls for a doctor is able to give correct information as to the location of the injured person. In order to help the physician to know what equipment may be needed in each particular case, the person making the call should give the doctor as much information about the injury as possible.

22. If nobody uses his head at the scene of an accident, there is danger that

    A. no one will get the names of all the witnesses
    B. a large crowd will gather
    C. the victim will not get the care he needs
    D. the victim will blame the City for negligence

23. When an accident occurs, the FIRST thing you should do is

    A. call a doctor
    B. loosen the clothing of the injured person
    C. notify the victim's family
    D. try to find out what is wrong with the injured person

24. If you do NOT know the extent and nature of the victim's injuries, you should

    A. let the injured person lie where he is
    B. immediately take the victim to a hospital yourself
    C. help the injured person to his feet to see if he can walk
    D. have the injured person sit up on the ground while you examine him

25. If the injured person is breathing and unconscious, you should

    A. get some hot liquid such as coffee or tea in to him
    B. give him artificial respiration
    C. lift up his head to try to stimulate blood circulation
    D. see that he lies flat on his back

26. If it is necessary to call a doctor, you should

    A. go and make the call yourself since you have all the information
    B. find out who the victim's family doctor is before making the call
    C. have someone else make the call who knows the location of the victim
    D. find out which doctor the victim can afford

27. It is important for the caller to give the doctor as much information as is available regarding the injury so that the doctor

    A. can bring the necessary equipment
    B. can make out an accident report
    C. will be responsible for any malpractice resulting from the first aid treatment
    D. can inform his nurse on how long he will be in the field

Questions 28-29.

DIRECTIONS: Questions 28 and 29 are to be answered SOLELY on the basis of the paragraph below.

When a written report must be submitted by an operator to his supervisor, the best rule is "the briefer the better." Obviously, this can be carried to extremes, since all necessary information must be included. However, the ability to write a satisfactory one-page report is an important communication skill. There are several different kinds of reports in common use. One is the form report, which is printed and merely requires the operator to fill in blanks. The greatest problems faced in completion of this report are accuracy and thoroughness. Another type of report is one that must be submitted regularly and systematically. This type of report is known as the periodic report.

28. According to the passage above, accuracy and thoroughness are the GREATEST problems in the completion of

    A. one-page reports   B. form reports
    C. periodic reports   D. long reports

29. According to the passage above, a good written report from an operator to his supervisor should be

    A. printed
    B. formal
    C. periodic
    D. brief

Question 30.

DIRECTIONS: The sketches below show 150-lb. chlorine cylinders stored in three different ways:

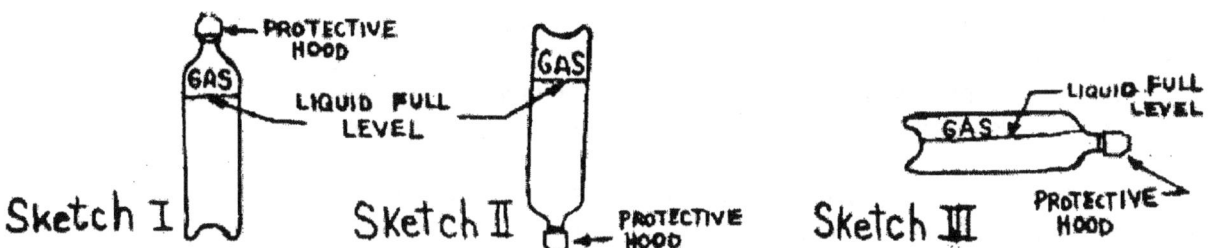

30. *Recommended* practice is to store a 150-lb. chlorine cylinder as shown in   30.____

    A. Sketch I *only*
    B. Sketch II *only*
    C. Sketch III *only*
    D. Sketches II and III

31. Of the following, the MOST serious defect in the installation shown below is that   31.____

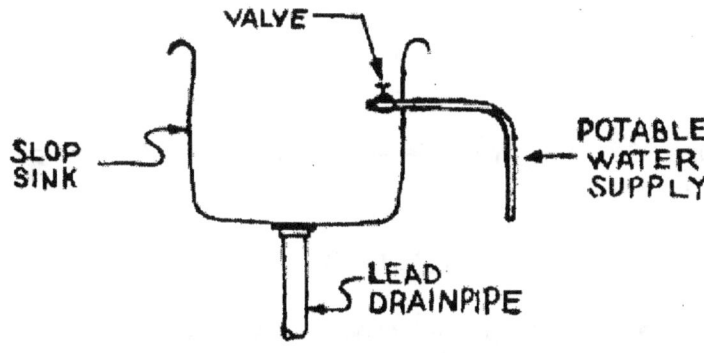

    A. the water supply should be directed downward to prevent excessive splashing over the rim
    B. the above installation may allow backflow of waste water into the water supply line
    C. lead pipes should not be used on drains from fixtures connected to the potable water supply
    D. excessive corrosion will occur on the valve if it becomes submerged

32. Of the following, the distance "x" which would be SAFEST when using the extension ladder shown in the sketch below is   32.____

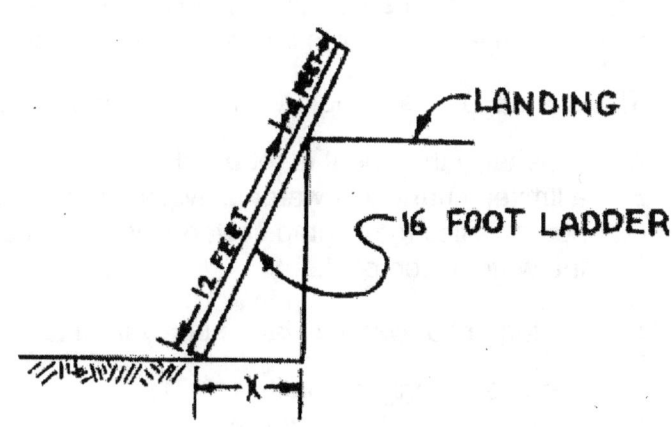

    A. 1 foot   B. 3 feet   C. 5 feet   D. 7 fee

33. Of the following statements regarding safe procedures for lifting a heavy object by yourself from the floor, the one which is FALSE is that

    A. you should keep your back as straight as possible
    B. you should bend your knees
    C. you should mainly use your back muscles in lifting
    D. your feet should be kept clear in case the object is dropped

34. It is generally not considered to be good practice to paint wood ladders. Of the following, the best reason for NOT painting wood ladders is that

    A. it may hide defects in the wood
    B. the rungs become slippery
    C. the hardware on the ladder becomes unworkable
    D. it would rub off on the surfaces against which it is resting

35. A rip saw would MOST likely be used to cut

    A. wood   B. steel   C. copper   D. aluminum

Questions 36-37.

DIRECTIONS: Questions 36 and 37 are to be answered SOLELY on the basis of the paragraph below.

NATURAL LAKES

Large lakes may yield water of exceptionally fine quality except near the shore line and in the vicinity of sewer outlets or near outlets of large streams. Therefore, minimum treatment is required. The availability of practically unlimited quantities of water is also a decided advantage. Unfortunately, however, the sewage from a city is often discharged into the same lake from which the water supply is taken. Great care must be taken in locating both the water intake and the sewer outlet so that the pollution handled by the water treatment plant is a minimum.

Sometimes the distance from the shore where dependable, satisfactory water can be found is so great that the cost of water intake facilities is prohibitive for a small municipality. In such cases, another supply must be found, or water must be obtained from a neighboring large city. Lake water is usually uniform in quality from day to day and does not vary in temperature as much as water from a river or small impounding reservoir.

36. A disadvantage of drawing a water supply from a large lake is that

    A. expensive treatment is required
    B. a limited quantity of water is available
    C. nearby cities may dump sewage into the lake
    D. the water is too cold.

37. An advantage of drawing a water supply from a large lake is that the

    A. water is uniform in quality
    B. water varies in temperature
    C. intake is distant from the shore
    D. intake may be near a sewer outlet

38. The *BEST* type of wrench to use to tighten a pipe without marring the pipe surface is   38.____

    A. pipe wrench
    B. strap wrench
    C. spanner wrench
    D. box wrench

39. Of the following statements concerning the use and care of files, the *one* which is *FALSE*   39.____
    is that

    A. files should have tight-fitting handles
    B. rasps are generally used on wood
    C. files should be protected by a light coating of oil when cutting metal
    D. files should be given a quick blow on a wood block to unclog teeth

40. A device which permits flow of a fluid in a pipe in one direction only is known as   40.____

    A. diode
    B. curb box
    C. gooseneck
    D. check valve

KEY (CORRECT ANSWERS)

1. D	11. B	21. B	31. B
2. A	12. A	22. C	32. B
3. A	13. A	23. D	33. C
4. D	14. D	24. A	34. A
5. C	15. C	25. D	35. A
6. B	16. D	26. C	36. C
7. B	17. A	27. A	37. A
8. C	18. D	28. B	38. B
9. D	19. D	29. D	39. C
10. C	20. A	30. A	40. D

TEST 2

DIRECTIONS: Each question or incomplete statement is followed by several suggested answers or completions. Select the one that *BEST* answers the question or completes the statement. *PRINT THE LETTER OF THE CORRECT ANSWER IN THE SPACE AT THE RIGHT.*

Questions 1-2.

DIRECTIONS: Questions 1 and 2 are to be answered *SOLELY* on the basis of the paragraph below.

PRECIPITATION AND RUNOFF

In the United States, the average annual precipitation is about 30 inches, of which about 21 inches is lost to the atmosphere by evaporation and transpiration. The remaining 9 inches becomes runoff into rivers and lakes. Both the precipitation and runoff vary greatly with geography and season. Annual precipitation varies from more than 100 inches in parts of the northwest to only 2 or 3 inches in parts of the southwest. In the northeastern part of the country, including New York State, the annual average precipitation is about 45 inches, of which about 22 inches becomes runoff. Even in New York State, there is some variation from place to place and considerable variation from time to time. During extremely dry years, the precipitation may be as low as 30 inches and the runoff below 10 inches. In general, there are greater variations in runoff rates from smaller watersheds. A critical water supply situation occurs when there are three or four abnormally dry years in succession.

Precipitation over the state is measured and recorded by a net- work of stations operated by the U. S. Weather Bureau. All of the precipitation records and other data such as temperature, humidity and evaporation rates are published monthly by the Weather Bureau in "Climatological Data." Runoff rates at more than 200 stream-gauging stations in the state are measured and recorded by the U. S. Geological Survey in cooperation with various state agencies. Records of the daily average flows are published annually by the U. S. Geological Survey in "Surface Water Records of New York." Copies may be obtained by writing to the Water Resources Division, United States Geological Survey, Albany, New York 23301.

1. From the above paragraphs it is *appropriate* to conclude that 1._____

   A. critical supply situations do not occur
   B. the greater the rainfall, the greater the runoff
   C. there are greater variations in runoff from larger watersheds
   D. the rainfall in the southwest is greater than the average in the country

2. From the above paragraphs, it is appropriate to conclude that 2._____

   A. an annual rainfall of about 50 inches does not occur in New York State
   B. the U. S. Weather Bureau is only interested in rainfall
   C. runoff is equal to rainfall less losses to the atmosphere
   D. information about rainfall and runoff in New York State is unavailable to the public

3. The following are diagrams of various types of bolt heads.

The *one* of the above which is a Phillips head type is the one labelled
A. A B. B C. C D. D

4. The appearance of frost on the outer surface of a chlorine cylinder which has been placed in service would MOST likely indicate that

A. the cylinder is empty
B. the gas is escaping too quickly from the cylinder
C. there is too much pressure in the cylinder
D. the humidity of the storage area is too high

5. One of the outer belts of a matched set of three V-belts becomes badly frayed. Of the following, the BEST course of action to take is to

A. replace only the worn belt
B. replace only the worn belt but put the new belt in the middle
C. remove the worn belt, put the center belt on the end and continue running the machine
D. replace the whole set of belts even if the other two belts show no signs of wear\

6. Of the following, the BEST type of valve to use for throttling or when the valve must be opened and closed frequently is a

A. check valve   B. globe valve
C. butterfly valve   D. pop valve

7. Of the following, the device which is used to measure *both* pressure and vacuum is the

A. compound gage   B. aquastat
C. pyrometer   D. thermocouple

8. Electrical energy is consumed and paid for in units of

A. voltage   B. ampere-hours
C. kilowatt-hours   D. watts

9. A "governor" on an engine is used to control the engine's

A. speed   B. temperature
C. interval of operation
D. engaging and disengaging the "load"

10. Pressure *below* that of the atmospheric pressure is usually expressed in

A. vacuum inches of mercury   B. inches of pressure absolute
C. BTU's   D. gallons per minute

11. A short piece of pipe with outside threads at both ends is called a

    A. union   B. nipple   C. tee   D. sleeve

12. Of the following, which device would MOST likely produce water hammer in a plumbing installation? A(n)

    A. relief valve
    B. air chamber
    C. surge tank
    D. quick-closing valve

13. Some portable electric tools have a third conductor in the line cord which is electrically connected to the receptacle box. The reason for this is to

    A. have a spare wire in case one power wire breaks
    B. protect the user of the tool from electrical shock
    C. strengthen the power lead so that it cannot be easily damaged
    D. allow use of the tool for extended periods of time without overheating

14. Of the following, the device which is usually used to measure the rate of flow of water in a pipe is a

    A. pressure gage
    B. Bourden gage
    C. manometer
    D. velocity meter

15. Acid, rosin fluid, or paste applied to metal surfaces to remove oxide film in preparation for soldering is known as

    A. grout   B. lampblack   C. plumber's soil   D. flux

16. In plumbing work, a coil spring which is inserted into a drain to facilitate cleaning of the drain is known as a

    A. pipe reamer   B. snake   C. plunger   D. spigot

17. Of the following, a pneumatic device is one that is driven or powered by

    A. air pressure
    B. oil pressure
    C. water pressure
    D. steam pressure

18. Of the following metals, the one which would MOST likely be used for an electric motor shaft is

    A. wrought iron
    B. hard bronze
    C. steel
    D. bras

19. Of the following, a rotary gear pump is BEST suited for pumping

    A. #6 fuel oil   B. hot water   C. sewage   D. kerosene

20. The MAIN reason for using a flexible coupling to join the shafts of two pieces of machinery together is that a flexible coupling

    A. allows for slight misalignment of the two shafts
    B. can be immediately disengaged in an emergency
    C. will automatically slip when overloaded thus protecting the driver machinery
    D. allows the driven load shaft to continue rotating under its own momentum, when the driver shaft is stopped

21. Of the following, the MAIN purpose of a house trap is to

   A. provide the house drain with a cleanout
   B. prevent gases from the public sewer from entering the house plumbing system
   C. trap articles of value that are accidentally dropped into the drainage pipes
   D. eliminate the necessity for traps under all other plumbing fixtures

21.____

22. Of the following, the MAIN reason for sometimes applying bituminous coating to the interiors of steel and cast-iron pipe is that this coating

   A. increases the tensile strength of the pipe
   B. increases the shock resistance of the pipe
   C. removes any objectionable taste from the water imparted by the pipe walls
   D. protects the pipe walls from corrosion

22.____

23. The one of the following electrical devices which is most likely to be used to raise or lower A.C. voltages is a

   A. resistor   B. thermistor   C. transformer   D. circuit-breaker

23.____

24. When a metal is galvanized, it is given a coating of

   A. nickel   B. tin   C. oxide   D. zinc

24.____

25. A conduit hickey is used to

   A. measure conduit pipe
   C. thread conduit pipe
   B. bend conduit pipe
   D. cut conduit pipe

25.____

Questions 26-27.

DIRECTIONS: Questions 26 and 27 are to be answered SOLELY on the basis of the electrical circuit shown below.

26. The circuit above is commonly known as a

   A. series circuit
   C. short circuit
   B. parallel circuit
   D. circuit breaker

26.____

27. The current flowing in the circuit above is

   A. 1 amp   B. 2 amps   C. 3 amps   D. 6 amps

27.____

Questions 28-30.

DIRECTIONS: Questions 28 to 30 inclusive are to be answered *SOLELY* on the basis of the sketches shown below.

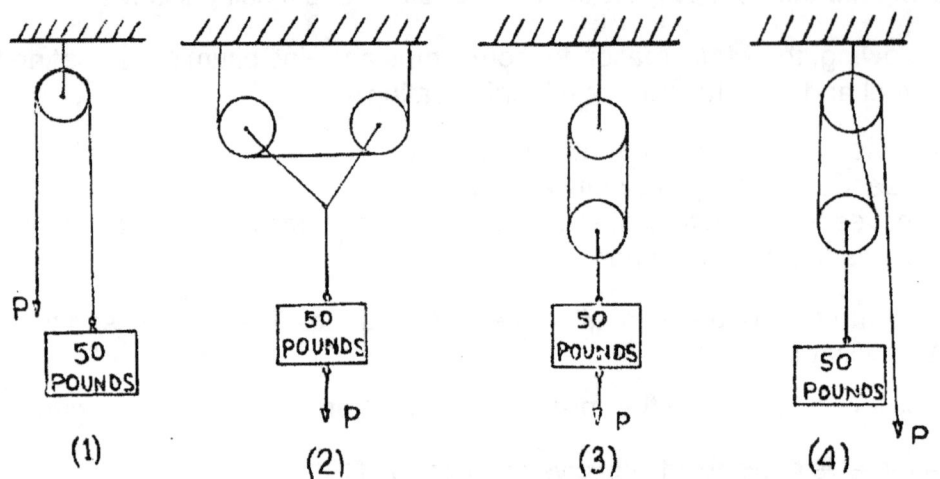

28. The two arrangements in the above diagrams which *CANNOT* be used to raise the load at all by applying a pull "p" as shown are setups

    A. 1 and 2 B. 2 and 3 C. 3 and 4 D. 1 and 4

29. The arrangement in the diagram above which requires the *LEAST* effort "p" to move the 50-pound weight is setup

    A. 1 B. 2 C. 3 D. 4

30. The effort required to hold the 50-pound weight at rest off the ground in setup (1) in the diagram above is

    A. 10 pounds B. 25 pounds C. 50 pounds D. 100 pounds

31. Of the following formulas, the one which *CORRECTLY* shows the relationship between gage pressure and absolute pressure is

    A. Absolute pressure = gage pressure / atmospheric pressure
    B. Absolute pressure + gage pressure = atmospheric pressure
    C. Absolute pressure = gage pressure + atmospheric pressure
    D. Absolute pressure + atmospheric pressure = gage pressure

32. The weight of a gallon of water is, most nearly,

    A. 8.3 pounds B. 16.6 pounds C. 24.9 pounds D. 33.2 pounds

33. Solenoid valves are usually operated

    A. thermally B. manually C. hydraulically D. electrically

34. A 1/2-inch, 8-32 round-head machine screw has

    A. a diameter of 1/2 inch
    B. a length of 8 inches
    C. 8 threads per inch
    D. 32 threads per inch

35. The MAIN purpose for the stuffing usually found in centrifugal pump stuffing boxes is

    A. supporting the shaft
    B. controlling the rate of discharge
    C. preventing fluid leakage
    D. compensating for shaft misalignment

36. The BEST wrench to use on screwed valves and fittings having hexagonal shape connections is the

    A. chain wrench
    B. open-end wrench
    C. pipe wrench
    D. strap wrench

37. A tap is a tool commonly used to

    A. remove broken screws
    B. flare pipe ends
    C. cut external threads
    D. cut internal threads

38. A thread chaser is MOST likely to be used to

    A. rethread damaged threads
    B. remove broken taps
    C. flare tubing
    D. adjust diestocks

39. If an air-conditioning unit shorted out and caught fire, the BEST fire extinguisher to use would be a

    A. water extinguisher
    B. foam extinguisher
    C. carbon dioxide extinguisher
    D. soda acid extinguisher

40. Of the following, the best action to take to help someone whose eyes have been splashed with lye is to FIRST

    A. wash out the eyes with clean water
    B. wash out the eyes with a salt water solution
    C. apply a sterile dressing over the eyes
    D. do nothing to the eyes, but telephone for medical help

KEY (CORRECT ANSWERS)

1. B	11. B	21. B	31. C
2. C	12. D	22. D	32. A
3. C	13. B	23. C	33. D
4. B	14. D	24. D	34. D
5. D	15. D	25. B	35. C
6. B	16. B	26. A	36. B
7. A	17. A	27. B	37. D
8. C	18. C	28. B	38. A
9. A	19. A	29. D	39. C
10. A	20. A	30. C	40. A

EXAMINATION SECTION
TEST 1

DIRECTIONS: Each question or incomplete statement is followed by several suggested answers or completions. Select the one that BEST answers the question or completes the statement. *PRINT THE LETTER OF THE CORRECT ANSWER IN THE SPACE AT THE RIGHT.*

Questions 1-5.

DIRECTIONS: Questions 1 through 5, inclusive, refer to the distribution map shown on the LAST page of this test. All questions are to be answered in accordance with this map.

1. The symbol just west of the boundary gate symbol on 21st Street between Willow Avenue and Meadow Avenue is a

   A. hydrant
   B. gate valve
   C. check valve
   D. reducer

2. The number of hydrants on the 30" main in Meadow Avenue between 22nd Street and 23rd Street is

   A. none   B. 1   C. 2   D. 3

3. The *S* symbol on the main at the west end of 18th Street means that the main is

   A. a special casting
   B. made of steel
   C. shut down
   D. high pressure service

4. A cap is located at or near the intersection of _____ Street and _____ Avenue.

   A. 24th; Willow
   B. 22nd; Willow
   C. 26th; Meadow
   D. 21st; Central

5. A blow off is located in

   A. Meadow Avenue between 19th & 20th Streets
   B. 22nd Street between Willow Avenue and Meadow Avenue
   C. Wilen Avenue between 22nd and 23rd Streets
   D. 22nd Street between Willow Avenue and Central Avenue

6. Assume that a normally sober man appears on the job intoxicated. Of the following, the BEST procedure for a foreman to follow is to

   A. give the man an easy job so that he cannot get hurt
   B. let the man *sleep it off* in the morning and put him to work in the afternoon
   C. let the man work at his normal duties but keep an *eye* on him
   D. send him home for the day

7. The Chief Engineer has decided to change the procedure that must be followed in making certain types of repairs. The one of the following statements concerning the new procedure that is CORRECT is:
The men

A. should know why the procedure is being changed because they will then be more interested in the job
B. do not have to know the reason for the change because they need do only the work as they are told
C. should know why the procedure is being changed so that they can decide which method of doing the job is better
D. do not have to know the reason for the change because they are not capable of judging the best method of doing a job

8. A foreman, by mistake, orders his men to do a job improperly.
Of the following, the BEST thing for the foreman to do when he realizes his error is to

   A. insist that the job be done as he ordered so that his mistake will not be discovered
   B. admit that he made the mistake and correct the order
   C. tell the men that the order came from *higher up* so that he will not be blamed for the mistake
   D. tell the men that he is merely trying this out to see if it works better

9. The BEST foreman is usually the

   A. fastest worker
   B. man who is most familiar with the streets in the borough
   C. strongest man
   D. man who is most tactful

10. A good foreman will

   A. look after the welfare of his men
   B. demand perfection in the work of his men at all times
   C. make special efforts to impress his superiors
   D. cover up for the actions of his men

11. As a newly appointed foreman, it is MOST important that you

   A. show the men who is boss by issuing orders
   B. prove to the men that you know more than they do
   C. become acquainted with the men and their abilities
   D. show the men how friendly you are

12. A foreman who criticizes his department head is a

   A. *good* foreman, because the men will feel he is on their side
   B. *poor* foreman, because the men will lose respect for him
   C. *good* foreman, because he will get more work done
   D. *poor* foreman, because he will have no time to do his own work

13. One of the men in your gang comes to you, the foreman, and complains that the men in the gang have taken a dislike to him and are making trouble for him.
Of the following, the BEST thing for you to do is to

   A. tell the man he must learn to get along with the other men
   B. report the matter to your superior
   C. call the gang together and tell them they must stop making trouble
   D. investigate the complaint to determine what the problem is

14. As a foreman, you are inspecting the damage done by water from a broken main leaking into the basement of a store. After inspecting the damage, the owner complains to you about the conduct of the men who made the repair.
Of the following, the BEST way of handling this situation is to tell the owner that

    A. you are there to inspect the damage to the premises only
    B. he should make his complaint to higher authorities
    C. his complaint will be investigated and, if found correct, proper action will be taken
    D. nothing can be done at this time since the men are no longer at this location

14_____

Questions 15-17.

DIRECTIONS: Questions 15 through 17, inclusive, are based on the paragraph below. These questions are to be answered in accordance with the information given in this paragraph.

Excavation of trench. The trench shall be excavated as directed; one side of the street or avenue shall be left open for traffic at all times. In paved streets, the length of trench that may be opened between the point where the backfilling has been completed and the point where the pavement is being removed shall not exceed fifteen hundred feet for pipes 24 inches or less in diameter. For pipes larger than 24 inch, the length of open trenches shall not exceed one thousand feet. The completion of the backfilling shall be interpreted to mean the backfilling of the trench and the consolidation of the backfill so that vehicular traffic can be resumed over the backfill, and also the placing of any temporary pavement that *may* be required.

15. According to the above paragraph, the street

    A. can be closed to traffic in emergencies
    B. can be closed to traffic only when laying more than 1500 feet of pipe
    C. is closed to traffic as directed
    D. shall be left open for traffic at all times

15_____

16. According to the above paragraph, the MAXIMUM length of open trench permitted in paved streets depends on the

    A. traffic on the street
    B. type of ground that is being excaVated
    C. water conditions met with in excavation
    D. diameter of the pipe being laid

16_____

17. According to the above paragraph, the one of the following items that is included in the *completion of the back-filling* is

    A. sheeting and bracing   B. cradle
    C. temporary pavement   D. bridging

17_____

Questions 18-20.

DIRECTIONS: Questions 18 through 20, inclusive, are based on the paragraph below. These questions are to be answered in accordance with the information given in this paragraph.

The Contractor shall notify the Engineer by noon of the day immediately preceding the date when he wishes to shut down any main, and if the time set be approved, the Contractor shall provide the men necessary to shut down the main at the time stipulated, and to previously notify all consumers whose supply may be affected. These men shall be under the direction of the Department employees, who will superintend all operations of valves and hydrants. Shutdowns for making connections will not be made unless and until the Contractor has everything on the ground in readiness for the work.

18. According to the above paragraph, before a contractor can make a shut-down, he MUST notify the

    A. Police Department
    B. district foreman
    C. engineer
    D. highway department

19. According to the above paragraph, the operation of the valves will be supervised by the

    A. department employees
    B. contractor's men
    C. contractor's superintendent
    D. engineer

20. According to the above paragraph, shut-downs for connections are made

    A. the day before the connection is made
    B. first and then consumers are notified
    C. at any time convenient to the contractor
    D. when the contractor has everything on the ground in readiness for the work

21. Water hammer in a pipe line is MOST frequently caused by _____ a valve too _____ .

    A. opening; rapidly
    B. opening; slowly
    C. closing; rapidly
    D. closing; slowly

22. In using a hacksaw, pressure should be applied to the hacksaw when

    A. pushing it
    B. pulling it
    C. pushing and pulling it
    D. either pushing or pulling, depending upon the way the cut is to be made

23. When cutting cast iron (other than pipe) with a hacksaw, the PROPER number of teeth per inch in the blade should be

    A. 14   B. 18   C. 24   D. 32

24. Concrete is a mixture of cement and

    A. lime, sand, and water
    B. sand and water
    C. sand and broken stone
    D. sand, broken stone, and water

25. The head of a cold chisel has mushroomed after considerable use.
The BEST thing to do is

   A. continue to use it since mushrooming is normal
   B. throw it away
   C. send it to the shop for redressing
   D. use a file to restore the head to its original shape

26. A valve box cover has been covered with asphalt during a street repaving job.
The BEST way to locate the valve is to use a

   A. geophone
   B. aquaphone
   C. distribution map and a tape
   D. probing bar

27. The number of cubic yards in a bin 4 feet by 8 feet by 13 feet is MOST NEARLY _____ cubic yards.

   A. 17   B. 15   C. 13   D. 11

28. The letter *P* stencilled on the roadside face of a hydrant indicates that the hydrant

   A. is a low pressure hydrant
   B. is a high pressure hydrant
   C. is out of service permanently
   D. has a plugged drain

29. A hydrant extension piece would MOST likely be used if

   A. the hydrant had been damaged
   B. an open trench exists in the street in front of the hydrant
   C. several hose lines must be connected to the hydrant
   D. the hose connections do not fit the hydrant nozzles

30. The drip valve of a hydrant

   A. should not open until after the hydrant valve has closed
   B. should open just before the hydrant valve has closed
   C. operates completely independent of the operation of the hydrant valve
   D. should only be closed during repair of the hydrant

31. To remove and replace the operating parts of a hydrant which is in service,

   A. the standpipe must be disconnected from the elbow
   B. it is necessary to do some excavating
   C. the main must be shut down
   D. no excavation is necessary

32. The material generally used for packing hydrant stems is

   A. asbestos   B. rubber cloth
   C. flax   D. leather

33. A roundabout would normally have as a component part a

    A. four-way   B. valve   C. plug   D. cap

34. Cast iron reducers are usually made in all but one of the following ways. The way in which they are NOT made is

    A. spigots on both ends
    B. hub on large end, spigot on small end
    C. hub on small end, spigot on large end
    D. hubs on both ends

35. A cast iron main running due east is to turn so that it runs N45W, that is, halfway between north and west. The change in direction could be made using _____ bends.

    A. sixteen 1/48   B. six 1/16
    C. four 1/8   D. two 1/4

36. A cast iron offset would NORMALLY be used

    A. to change the direction of a main
    B. when the main must run diagonally from one side of the street to the other
    C. when the main must be shifted parallel to itself several feet to avoid an existing structure
    D. when the main must be shifted several inches to avoid an existing structure

37. A 30-inch cast iron main is to be laid with a blow-off and an air cock. The cast iron piece used for the blow-off differs from that used for the air cock in

    A. size of outlet
    B. general shape
    C. material used
    D. length measured along the main

38. The upper part of a standard hydrant valve box is USUALLY connected to the lower part by

    A. screw threads   B. bolts
    C. a beaded rim   D. lugs and rods

39. A trench for an 18-inch cast iron main is being excavated in rock. The width of the trench should be AT LEAST _____ inches.

    A. 30   B. 36   C. 42   D. 48

40. Specifications of the Department of Water Supply, Gas and Electricity state that in a trench excavated in rock, projections of rock must be removed if they come within a certain distance of the outside of any portion of the pipe barrel or bell. This distance is, in inches,

    A. 4   B. 6   C. 8   D. 10

KEY (CORRECT ANSWERS)

1. D	11. C	21. C	31. D
2. A	12. B	22. A	32. C
3. B	13. D	23. B	33. B
4. D	14. C	24. D	34. D
5. D	15. D	25. C	35. B
6. D	16. D	26. C	36. D
7. A	17. C	27. B	37. A
8. B	18. C	28. D	38. A
9. D	19. A	29. B	39. C
10. A	20. D	30. A	40. B

8 (#1)

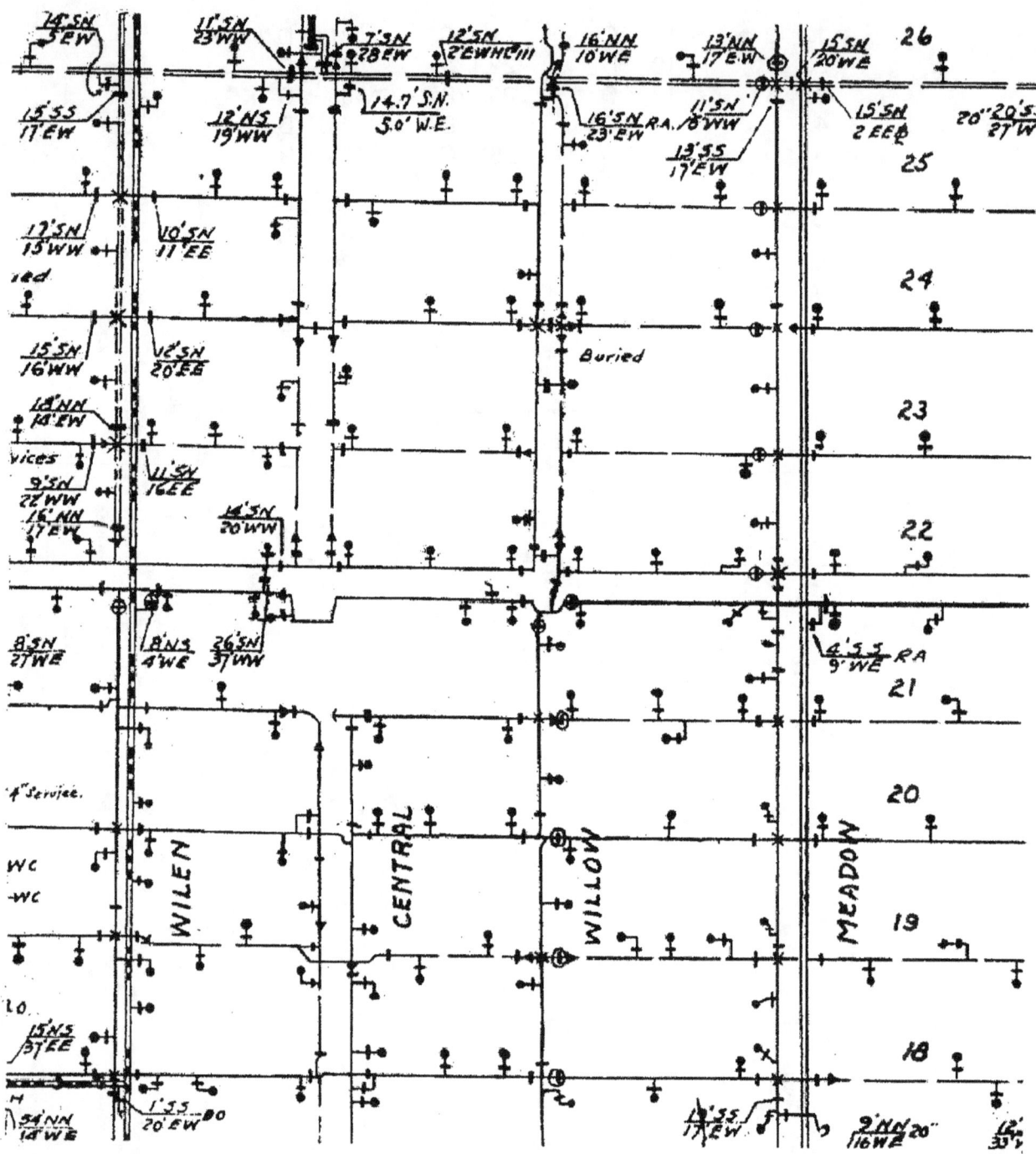

TEST 2

DIRECTIONS: Each question or incomplete statement is followed by several suggested answers or completions. Select the one that BEST answers the question or completes the statement. *PRINT THE LETTER OF THE CORRECT ANSWER IN THE SPACE AT THE RIGHT.*

1. The MAXIMUM size of stones permitted in backfill is _____ inches.

    A. 12   B. 8   C. 4   D. 2

    1_____

2. A two-inch galvanized steel pipe is to be connected to a cast iron main.
The connection should be made by a standard corporation tap of the following size: _____ inch.

    A. 1   B. 1 1/2   C. 2   D. 2 1/2

    2_____

3. Standard cast iron pipe of inside diameter from 12 to 20 inches may be furnished in nominal laying lengths up to and including _____ feet.

    A. 14   B. 16   C. 18   D. 20

    3_____

4. The interior surface of new 12-inch cast iron pipe is USUALLY coated with

    A. cement mortar B. nothing
    C. asphalt paint D. coal tar pitch

    4_____

5. A tarpaulin would MOST likely be used when

    A. mixing concrete
    B. running lead joints
    C. lowering pipe into a trench
    D. excavating a trench for a water main

    5_____

6. Bands and bolts would be LEAST likely to be required at

    A. bends   B. branches   C. plugs   D. four-ways

    6_____

7. A house service with a 3/8-inch tap on an existing main is to be transferred to a new main.
The size of the tap on the new main should be _____ inch.

    A. 5/8   B. 1/2   C. 3/8   D. 1/4

    7_____

8. The LARGEST tap permitted on a new 12-inch main is _____ inch.

    A. 1   B. 1 1/2   C. 2   D. 2 1/2

    8_____

9. The sheeting of a trench serves

    A. only to protect workmen
    B. only to prevent damage to existing mains close to the trench
    C. only to prevent damage to pavement
    D. all three of the foregoing purposes

    9_____

10. Water required for flushing backfill is USUALLY supplied

    A. in a fine spray
    B. by an ordinary garden hose
    C. from a tank truck
    D. through a flushing pipe

11. Water mains are USUALLY laid parallel to the curb at a distance of APPROXIMATELY _____ feet.

    A. 15　　B. 12　　C. 9　　D. 6

12. After a main has been laid but prior to putting it into service, it should be disinfected by

    A. continuous flushing with water containing chlorine
    B. continuous flushing with clean water only
    C. introducing chlorine into the water in the pipe and letting the solution stand for 30 minutes
    D. blowing chlorine gas through the main

13. Before trimming a caulked pipe joint, the lead of a lead joint should

    A. extend outside the face of the bell
    B. be flush with the face of the bell
    C. be inside the face of the bell
    D. be heated

14. Drainage of hydrants require the use of lead lined pipe

    A. except when a cast iron drain base is provided
    B. except when the hydrant is connected to a sewer
    C. except when a blind drain is provided
    D. in every case

15. A standard cast iron reducer is to connect a 24-inch main to a smaller main. The length of the reducer USUALLY

    A. is the same regardless of the size of the smaller main
    B. decreases as the size of the smaller main decreases
    C. increases as the size of the smaller main decreases
    D. can be varied to fit the field conditions

16. A standard cast iron three-way does NOT have more than the following number of hubs:

    A. 3　　B. 2　　C. 1　　D. 0

17. Of the following statements, the one which is CORRECT is:

    A. A cap is used on the spigot end of a pipe
    B. A plug is used on the spigot end of a pipe
    C. Caps and plugs can be used interchangeably
    D. Caps are usually available in larger sizes than plugs

18. Of the following statements, the one which is CORRECT is:

    A. A planned shutdown is not made rapidly
    B. In the event of an emergency shutdown, all valves in the area should be closed and then a study of the distribution map should be made to determine which valves can be opened
    C. Boundary gates should always be kept closed for the duration of an emergency shutdown
    D. The operation of all valves to be used in a planned shutdown should be checked prior to making the shutdown

19. When building material is stored on the street for the construction of a building,

    A. the Department of Water Supply, Gas and Electricity is not concerned
    B. there can be no objections if hydrants are accessible
    C. there can be no objections if the storage period is short
    D. serious difficulties for the Department of Water Supply, Gas and Electricity could result

20. A large steel main is to be emptied through a blow-off. The BEST way to proceed is to open

    A. the blow-off
    B. an aircock or hydrant at the high point of the main before opening the blow-off
    C. the blow-off and then open an air cock or hydrant at the high point of the main
    D. an air cock or hydrant at the low point of the main before opening the blow-off

21. A large new main is to be placed in service.
    To fill the main, it is important to FIRST open

    A. the head gate valve
    B. an air cock or hydrant on the main
    C. all side gate valves
    D. the side gate valves on one side of the main only

22. Of the following special castings, the one which is MOST like a blow-off is a

    A. four-way   B. reducer   C. three-way   D. offset

23. The laying length of a double hub

    A. is less than one foot
    B. depends upon the diameter of the pipe
    C. must be at least nine feet
    D. may be any length up to 20 feet, the maximum length depending upon the diameter

24. The gooseneck that is GENERALLY used to connect a service pipe to a main

    A. should be straight for its entire length
    B. comes in a standard length and, therefore, must be curved to make it fit

C. is deliberately curved so that it can accommodate movement between main and service pipe
D. is curved to provide extra length so that it can be cut and still be long enough to reconnect to the main

25. A non-rising stem gate valve would MOST likely be used when

   A. the threads of the stem must be readily accessible for lubrication
   B. space is limited
   C. the valve is used infrequently
   D. the valve is in a deep valve vault

26. Of the following types of valves, the one which is NOT usually found on water mains is the _____ valve.

   A. glove   B. air relief
   C. pressure regulating   D. gate

27. When a length of cast iron pipe is too long, it is USUALLY cut with a(n)

   A. chisel   B. hacksaw
   C. emery wheel   D. cutting torch

28. The PRINCIPAL objection to laying mains between December 15 and March 15 is with the

   A. freezing of water
   B. working conditions for the men
   C. freezing of soil
   D. the reduced length of daylight

29. A trench for a cast iron main is USUALLY backfilled immediately

   A. after the joints are caulked
   B. after the pressure test has been completed
   C. before water is placed in the main
   D. after water is placed in the main

30. When the pavement along the sides of a trench becomes undermined, the BEST thing to do is

   A. carefully tamp the backfill under the undermined pavement
   B. place a layer of broken stone on top of the backfill under the undermined pavement
   C. break down the undermined pavement before backfilling
   D. consolidate the backfill by thorough flushing

31. A small leak in a main would usually be MOST serious in the

   A. summer   B. fall   C. spring   D. winter

32. When sheeting for a trench is not to be removed before backfilling, the sheeting should be driven or cut off so that it

   A. is flush with the surface of the ground
   B. is at least 8 inches below the surface of the ground

C. will project at least two inches into the pavement base
D. is flush with the top surface of the pavement base

33. While excavating a trench in rock by blasting, a water main which crosses the line of the trench is uncovered. Of the following methods, the BEST one for continuing the rock excavation in the vicinity of the main is

   A. shut down the main
   B. place blasting mats to cover the main
   C. use lighter blasting charges
   D. relocate the main temporarily so that it is outside the danger area of the building

34. When the bottom of a trench for a water main is in rock, the pipe should be permanently supported on

   A. clean earth backfill which is tamped
   B. wooden blocking
   C. sand backfill which is flushed
   D. concreted cradles

35. On which one of the following days of the week should a planned shutdown normally be made?

   A. Sunday   B. Monday
   C. Tuesday   D. Wednesday

36. Permissible leakage during a field test is two (2) gallons per linear foot of pipe joint per 24 hours.
   For a 24-inch main, 1,000 feet long, with 16-foot laying lengths, the permissible leakage in 24 hours is, in gallons, MOST NEARLY

   A. 750   B. 770   C. 790   D. 810

37. Contract limitations on the maximum quantities of materials that may be delivered to the site, and on the time of such deliveries, are USUALLY made in order to

   A. insure the completion of the work on schedule
   B. prevent the contractor from asking for an extension of time because materials were not available
   C. reduce congestion at the site of the work
   D. protect the manufacturer supplying the material

38. Steel reinforcing bars for reinforced concrete should

   A. be painted with red lead
   B. be painted with asphalt paint
   C. be painted with oil paint
   D. not be painted

39. Steel water mains are lined with

   A. coal tar enamel only
   B. coal tar enamel or cement mortar
   C. cement mortar only
   D. nothing

40. The principal danger in NOT opening an air cock when draining a main is that the main might

   A. not empty
   B. only partly empty
   C. empty too fast
   D. collapse

KEY (CORRECT ANSWERS)

1. C	11. C	21. B	31. D
2. B	12. A	22. C	32. B
3. D	13. A	23. A	33. D
4. A	14. D	24. C	34. D
5. C	15. C	25. B	35. D
6. D	16. B	26. A	36. C
7. A	17. A	27. A	37. C
8. C	18. D	28. C	38. D
9. D	19. D	29. A	39. B
10. D	20. B	30. C	40. D

EXAMINATION SECTION
TEST 1

DIRECTIONS: Each question or incomplete statement is followed by several suggested answers or completions. Select the one that BEST answers the question or completes the statement. *PRINT THE LETTER OF THE CORRECT ANSWER IN THE SPACE AT THE RIGHT.*

1. A Bourdon tube gage is used to measure

    A. temperature
    B. acidity
    C. turbidity
    D. pressure

    1._____

2. An instrument used to locate buried metallic pipes is known as a(n)

    A. scleroscope
    B. M-scope
    C. kinoscope
    D. oscilloscope

    2._____

3. The PRIMARY function of a check valve is to

    A. prevent the illegal use of fire hydrants
    B. insure adequate water pressure in high buildings
    C. prevent freezing of water
    D. permit flow of water in one direction only

    3._____

4. Of the following, the torque applied by a ratchet wrench would be expressed in units of

    A. horsepower
    B. pounds
    C. pounds per square inch
    D. foot-pounds

    4._____

5. Most lead joints runners are made of

    A. nylon
    B. asbestos
    C. leadite
    D. polyethylene

    5._____

6. The tool shown in the sketch at the right is a

    A. pickout iron
    B. pipe jointer
    C. cover bolt wrench
    D. pipe reamer

    6._____

7. In order to reduce the force necessary to open or close large gate valves, the valves are equipped with a

    A. vacuum breaker
    B. by-pass
    C. saddle
    D. shear gate

    7._____

8. In order to open a ground-key valve, used as a corporation cock to full flow, it is necessary to rotate the handle _____ degrees.

    A. 45   B. 60   C. 75   D. 90

    8._____

43

9. A foot valve is MOST often used

    A. to relieve excess pressure in a water main
    B. on the suction pipe of a centrifugal pump
    C. at the high point in a pipeline
    D. to drain a pipeline

10. Of the following tools, the one that generally should NOT be used to tighten screwed piping is a _____ wrench.

    A. Stillson
    B. strap
    C. monkey
    D. chain

11. A 6-inch branch may be connected to an 8-inch main without shutting off the flow of water by using a

    A. tapping valve and sleeve
    B. cutting in tee
    C. cutting in valve and sleeve
    D. pipe tong

12. When water flows through a thirty-second bend, the direction of flow changes

    A. 11 1/4°   B. 22 1/2°   C. 45°   D. 90°

13. A main in which water is flowing east is connected to a pipe offset.
    As the water leaves the offset, it will be flowing toward the

    A. north   B. south   C. east   D. west

14. An electrolysis test connection on a water main is used to measure the

    A. salinity of the ground water outside the main
    B. the chlorine residual in the water in the main
    C. stray electric current in the main
    D. temperature of the ground around the main

15. A common method of temporarily lowering the ground water below the level of operations in a trench is by the use of

    A. wellpoints
    B. mud valves
    C. piles
    D. trenching machines

16. The diameter of a #6 steel reinforcing bar is MOST NEARLY

    A. 1"   B. 3/4"   C. 1/2"   D. 1/4"

17. The quick opening or closing of valves or gates, and the sudden starting, stopping, or variation in speed of pumps is FREQUENTLY the cause of

    A. sluggish flow of water
    B. water-borne diseases
    C. water hammer
    D. water hardness

18. Poured lead pipe joints must be calked MAINLY because the hot lead

    A. corrodes some of the cast iron
    B. burns some of the jute
    C. becomes porous on cooling
    D. shrinks on cooling

19. Flexibility between a water main and a service pipe can be obtained by the use of a

    A. corporation cock
    B. gooseneck
    C. curb stop
    D. air-release valve

20. It is necessary to shut off the water in a main temporarily in order to make repairs. In order to get cooperation from the general public, the

    A. job should be done at night so that few people will be aware of it
    B. shut-off crew should be ordered not to speak to the general public
    C. job should be done in several stages so that the public realizes how difficult the problem is
    D. purpose and duration of the shut-off should be explained to the general public

Questions 21-25.

DIRECTIONS: Questions 21 through 25 are to be answered on the basis of maps or diagrams used by departments of water resources.

21. On a distribution map, the symbol ⎯⎯⎯ — ⎯⎯⎯ refers to a main whose diameter is

    A. 6"   B. 8"   C. 10"   D. 12"

22. On a distribution map, the symbol ⚲ refers to a

    A. gate valve
    B. blow-off
    C. air-cock
    D. regulator

23. On a distribution map, the symbol ⎯┼⎯ refers to a

    A. gate valve
    B. 3-way
    C. 4-way
    D. reducer

24. On a distribution map, the symbol ↓ refers to a

    A. hydrant   B. air-cock   C. 3-way   D. 4-way

25. On a work area diagram, the symbol ▨ refers to a(n)

    A. office
    B. truck
    C. barricade
    D. excavation.

KEY (CORRECT ANSWERS)

1. D
2. B
3. D
4. D
5. B

6. D
7. B
8. D
9. B
10. C

11. A
12. A
13. C
14. C
15. A

16. B
17. C
18. D
19. B
20. D

21. B
22. B
23. A
24. C
25. D

TEST 2

DIRECTIONS: Each question or incomplete statement is followed by several suggested answers or completions. Select the one that BEST answers the question or completes the statement. *PRINT THE LETTER OF THE CORRECT ANSWER IN THE SPACE AT THE RIGHT.*

1. According to standard water main specifications, prior to laying any straight pipe or special castings, the inside surfaces shall be mopped or sprayed with a chlorine solution containing not less than 150 _____ of chlorine.

    A. quarts   B. lbs.   C. p.p.m.   D. tanks

    1.____

2. When water main repairs are underway on the north side of a two-way street which runs east and west, the location recommended by the Department of Water Resources of a lead heating burner is _____ of the excavation.

    A. north   B. east   C. south   D. west

    2.____

3. Of the following statements, the one which is NOT included on the official water supply shut-off notice is

    A. turn off water-cooled refrigerating and air conditioning units
    B. close main house valve on water pipe supplying premises
    C. drain all water pipes above the basement
    D. open, as a vent, one hot water faucet above the level of the hot water storage tank

    3.____

4. In order to obtain a Temporary Street Opening Permit, the applicant must be a

    A. city resident   B. city employee
    C. licensed plumber   D. professional engineer

    4.____

5. In accordance with standard water main specifications, all water mains 20 inches in diameter or larger shall be subjected to a leakage test at a pressure of 125 psi. The leakage shall NOT be greater than

    A. twenty gallons per 24 hours
    B. two gallons per linear foot of pipe joint per 24 hours
    C. two gallons per linear foot of pipe joint per 20 minutes
    D. twenty gallons per mile of pipe per 24 hours

    5.____

6. In accordance with official specifications, in paved streets the length of trench that may be opened between the point where the backfilling has been completed and the point where the pavement is being removed shall NOT exceed

    A. the width of the street
    B. fifteen hundred feet for pipes 24 inches or less in diameter
    C. five hundred feet for all pipe diameters
    D. the distance between hydrants

    6.____

Questions 7-10.

DIRECTIONS: Questions 7 through 10 are to be answered SOLELY on the basis of the following passage.

47

The choice of equipment to be used in excavating a trench will depend on the job conditions, the depth and width of the trench, the class of the soil, the extent to which ground water is present, the width of the right of way for the disposal of excavated earth, and the type of equipment already owned by a contractor.

If a relatively shallow and narrow trench is to be excavated in firm soil, the wheel-type trenching machine is probably the most suitable. However, if the soil is rock, which requires blasting, the most suitable excavator will be a hoe, or a less desirable substitute could be a dragline. If the soil is unstable, water-saturated material, it may be necessary to use a dragline, hoe, or clamshell and let the walls establish a stable slope. If it is necessary to install solid sheeting to hold the walls in place, neither a hoe nor a dragline will work satisfactorily. A clamshell, which can excavate between the trench braces that hold the sheeting in place, probably will be the best equipment for the job.

7. According to the above passage, the wheel-type trenching machine is probably the MOST suitable for excavating

   A. unstable, water-saturated material
   B. when it is necessary to install solid sheeting
   C. a relatively shallow and narrow trench in firm soil
   D. when ground water is present

8. According to the above passage, the width of the right of way for the disposal of excavated earth

   A. depends upon the width of the street
   B. affects the depth of cover
   C. affects the choice of equipment to be used in excavating
   D. should be minimized to avoid inconveniencing the public

9. According to the above passage, a hoe will be the MOST suitable excavator if the

   A. soil is rock which requires blasting
   B. equipment is already owned by a contractor
   C. trench requires solid sheeting
   D. trench is over twenty feet deep

10. According to the above passage, the BEST equipment to use for excavating when it is necessary to install solid sheeting to hold the walls in place probably will be a

    A. clamshell
    B. dragline
    C. hoe
    D. wheel-type trenching machine

Questions 11-12.

DIRECTIONS: Questions 11 and 12 are to be answered SOLELY on the basis of the following passage.

Construction pumps frequently are required to perform under severe conditions, such as resulting from variations in the pumping head or from handling water that is muddy, sandy and trashy, or highly corrosive. The rate of pumping may vary several hundred percent during the period of construction. The most satisfactory solution to the pumping problem may be a single all-purpose pump, or it may be to use several types and sizes of pumps, to permit flexibility in the operations. The proper solution is to select the equipment which will take care of the pumping needs adequately at the lowest total cost.

11. According to the above passage, the PROPER solution to a construction pumping problem is to select equipment that has the lowest total cost which will also

    A. perform under severe conditions
    B. take care of the pumping needs adequately
    C. permit flexibility in operations
    D. provide maximum safety

12. According to the above passage, a variation of several hundred percent during the period of construction may occur in the

    A. pumping head
    B. rate of pumping
    C. volume of sandy and trashy water
    D. volume of highly corrosive water

Questions 13-14.

DIRECTIONS: Questions 13 and 14 are to be answered SOLELY on the basis of the following passage.

The mechanical failure of equipment may be the cause of a serious accident. Competent maintenance of equipment will reduce mechanical failures and in so doing reduce injuries and construction interruptions. Regular inspection of equipment will reduce maintenance expense.

13. Of the following, the BEST title for the above passage is

    A. Construction Productivity
    B. Preventive Maintenance of Equipment
    C. Inspection of Equipment
    D. Economical Construction

14. According to the above passage, the way to save money in construction work is to

    A. have qualified people operate equipment
    B. have periodic inspection of equipment
    C. have regular overhaul of equipment
    D. start a maintenance training program

15. Of the following items, the one MOST suitable for measuring the flow of water in a pipe is a

    A. poppet   B. hydraulic ram
    C. cistern   D. pitometer

16.

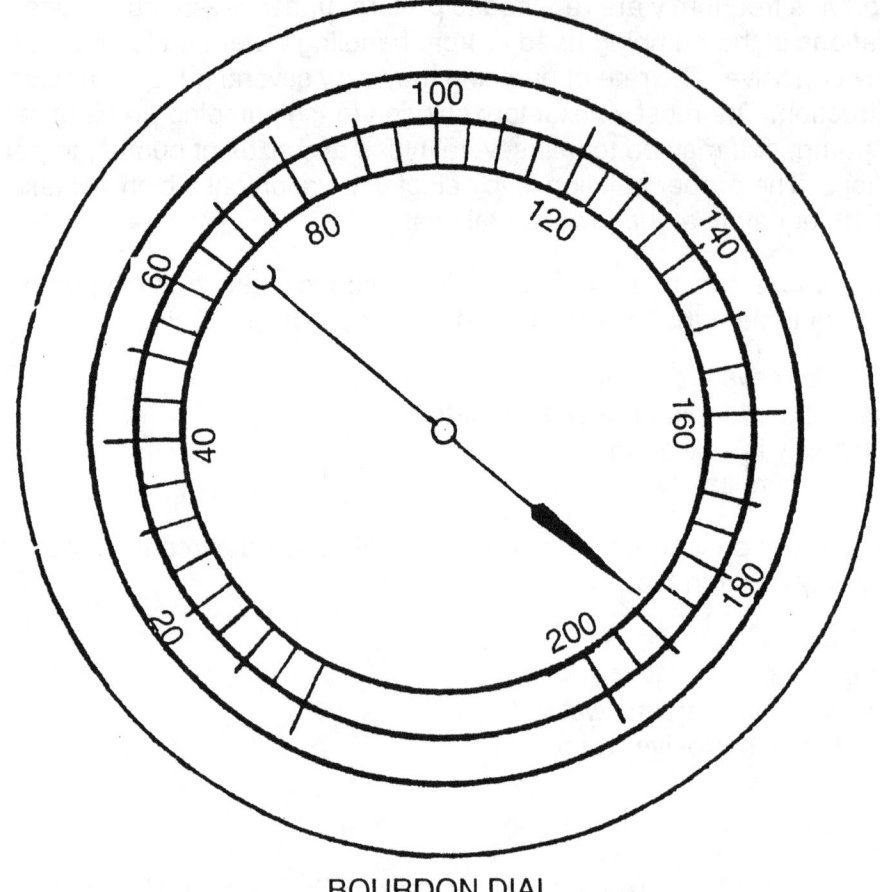

BOURDON DIAL

The reading indicated on the above dial is MOST NEARLY

A. 183 B. 188 C. 192 D. 196

17. An instrument used for detecting the sound of flowing water in a pipe network is a(n)

    A. micrometer B. spectrometer
    C. aquaphone D. viscophone

18. Of the following, the MAIN purpose of a Venturi meter is to measure the _____ in a main.

    A. quantity of water flowing
    B. chlorine content of the water
    C. velocity of the water
    D. temperature of the water

19. A blade with a small hole in the tip, used for measuring the flow from a hydrant, is a

    A. hydrant pitot B. Venturi meter
    C. parshall flume D. hydrant head

20. Hydrant-flow tests include observation of the pressure at a centrally situated hydrant and measurement of

    A. pressure at a group of neighboring hydrants
    B. flow from outlets at the top floor of a building
    C. reservoir elevation
    D. flow from a group of neighboring hydrants

21. Of the following, the one which is NOT a requirement of a satisfactory report is that it should be

    A. timely   B. lengthy   C. legible   D. accurate

22. When an accident occurs, the FIRST concern of the Foreman should be to

    A. see that injured person is properly cared for
    B. make sketches of the area
    C. interview the injured person
    D. interview witnesses and coworkers

23. Workers whose characteristics and behavior are such as to make them considerably more liable to injury than the average person are considered to be

    A. late
    B. safety conscious
    C. careful
    D. accident-prone

24. Safety inspections are not useful in an accident prevention program unless

    A. all persons who have accidents are fined
    B. insurance rates are decreased
    C. immediate action is taken to correct the conditions revealed
    D. there is adequate compensation for all injured parties

25. A Foreman is BEST qualified to investigate accidents involving his subordinates because he

    A. has all safety equipment for the job
    B. has more free time than his superiors
    C. has more skill than his superiors
    D. is familiar with all the job conditions

KEY (CORRECT ANSWERS)

1.	C	11.	B
2.	D	12.	B
3.	C	13.	B
4.	C	14.	B
5.	B	15.	D
6.	B	16.	B
7.	C	17.	C
8.	C	18.	A
9.	A	19.	A
10.	A	20.	D

21. B
22. A
23. D
24. C
25. D

EXAMINATION SECTION

TEST 1

DIRECTIONS: Each question or incomplete statement is followed by several suggested answers or completions. Select the one that BEST answers the question or completes the statement. *PRINT THE LETTER OF THE CORRECT ANSWER IN THE SPACE AT THE RIGHT.*

1. The MAIN advantage of a rotary pump over a centrifugal pump is that it   1._____
    A. has more velocity
    B. has greater speed
    C. delivers more gallons per minute
    D. is self-priming and requires no valves

2. Pump efficiency can be termed   2._____
    I. hydraulic   II. volumetric   III. thermal   IV. mechanical

    The CORRECT answer is:
    A. I, II   B. I, III, IV   C. I, II, IV   D. I, II, III, IV

3. A superheater vent valve is installed on a boiler to   3._____
    A. insure a flow of steam through the superheater when steam is being raised on the boiler
    B. insure that some of the excess steam is released
    C. lower the steam temperature
    D. none of the above

4. Which of the following is a wearing ring on a centrifugal pump?   4._____
    A. Lantern   B. Turbine   C. Impeller   D. Thrust

5. Worn sealing rings can cause the   5._____
    A. capacity to increase
    B. discharge to flow back into the inlet
    C. priming to stop
    D. shaft to throw out of alignment

6. Vibration is caused by   6._____
    A. packing too tight   B. water hammer
    C. shaft alignment   D. worn bearings

7. A condensate pump helps to   7._____
    A. create vacuum in the system
    B. induce the steam to circulate rapidly
    C. return the condensate back to the boiler
    D. reduce the back pressure on the engine

8. Important pumps on a feedwater line are the   8.._____
    I. rotary   II. vacuum   III. turbine   IV. centrifugal
    The CORRECT answer is:
    A. I, II   B. II, III, IV   C. I, II, III   D. I, II, III, IV

9. Which of the following is a reciprocating pump?
   A. Two stage
   B. Turbine
   C. Simplex
   D. All of the above

10. Which cylinder is larger on a duplex pump?
    A. Water
    B. Air
    C. Steam
    D. All are the same size

11. The FEWEST number of valves on a duplex pump is
    A. 4   B. 8   C. 12   D. 16

12. A pump may fail to discharge when the
    A. pump is not properly primed
    B. inlet valve is stuck
    C. valve seats are in bad condition
    D. all of the above

13. A pump may pound and vibrate because of
    A. air in the liquid
    B. a leaky inlet line
    C. excessive speed
    D. all of the above

14. If a pump races while increasing its output, the cause may be
    A. a leaky plunger
    B. a broken or stuck water valve
    C. an air leak
    D. not enough steam to move the piston

15. If the piston strikes the head of the cylinder, the cause would MOST probably be
    A. improper adjustment of the cushion valve
    B. cylinder rings are worn
    C. too much lap on the valves
    D. none of the above

16. To adjust the cushion valve, you should
    A. run the pump at full speed
    B. cut down the steam supply
    C. run the pump with a full load
    D. run the pump without a water load

17. If the pump lacks a cushion valve, you should
    A. lower the steam pressure
    B. adjust the lost motion enough to permit the pump to make a full stroke without striking
    C. adjust the piston rings
    D. adjust the back pressure valve

18. What condition would cause a piston to stop on dead center?
    A. The slide valve is worn
    B. There is not enough steam pressure
    C. There is too high of a head
    D. The cylinder shoulders are worn

19. Positive suction head is a condition present when the
    A. pump is located below the liquid supply
    B. pump is located between the boiler and the feedwater tank
    C. pump is located above the liquid supply
    D. water pressure is greater than the suction pressure

20. A centrifugal pump will most likely fail if
    A. the suction side of the pump is defective
    B. the discharge valve is closed
    C. wearing rings are worn
    D. strainer is clogged

21. The pump may fail to discharge if there is
    A. not enough water pressure
    B. improper priming
    C. air trapped at the top of the casing causing the pump to lose its discharge
    D. too high of a head

22. The failure of a pump to discharge can be rectified by
    A. increasing the water pressure
    B. reducing the pipe size
    C. decreasing the water pressure
    D. repriming the pump

23. To prevent a pump from failing to discharge, you should
    A. install a lantern ring
    B. replace the impeller
    C. install a bigger motor
    D. remove some packing

24. Reduction in both capacity and head is caused by
    A. too much air leaking through the packing
    B. reverse rotation of the motor
    C. a closed suction valve
    D. a clogged strainer

25. Small by-pass lines are installed around a large gate valve in order to
    A. equalize the pressure on the globe valve
    B. balance the pressure on the gate valve when the valve is being opened
    C. increase the velocity of the steam
    D. eliminate the sudden change in temperature of the steam

KEY (CORRECT ANSWERS)

1. D	11. B
2. D	12. D
3. A	13. D
4. C	14. D
5. B	15. A
6. D	16. D
7. C	17. B
8. D	18. A
9. C	19. A
10. C	20. A

21. B
22. D
23. A
24. B
25. B

TEST 2

DIRECTIONS: Each question or incomplete statement is followed by several suggested answers or completions. Select the one that BEST answers the question or completes the statement. *PRINT THE LETTER OF THE CORRECT ANSWER IN THE SPACE AT THE RIGHT.*

1. The purpose of a volume casing on a centrifugal pump is to
   A. convert velocity into vacuum
   B. convert velocity into pressure
   C. prevent cavitation of the pump
   D. increase the velocity of the water

   1.____

2. How many type of feedwater heaters are currently in existence
   A. 1   B. 2   C. 4   D. 5

   2.____

3. Which of the following are types of feedwater heaters?
   A. Economizer   B. Closed   C. Deaerator   D. All of the above

   3.____

4. When the temperature leaving the feedwater heater is too low, the MAIN problem is probably that
   A. steam pressure is too low
   B. back pressure is too low
   C. steam is of poor quality
   D. too much condensate is in the steam

   4.____

5. The advantage of a feedwater heater is:
   A. Hotter feedwater
   B. Less fuel consumption
   C. Less air in the feedwater
   D. All of the above

   5.____

6. To increase the back pressure, you should
   A. install a bigger back pressure valve
   B. put a heavier spring on the valve
   C. close the back pressure valve
   D. increase the line pressure

   6.____

7. Which of the following is NOT a use of a feedwater heater? To
   A. pre-heat the feedwater
   B. eliminate scale foaming substances by precipitation
   C. utilize some of the steam going to waste
   D. store generated steam

   7.____

8. In relation to the feedwater pump, the feedwater heater should be located
   A. in another part of the building
   A. in the basement of the plant
   B. about 10 or 12 feet above the pump

   8.____

57

9. An open feedwater heater is a heater
   A. open at one end
   B. with steam coils
   C. where water and steam are in actual contact
   D. with 2/3 steam space

10. The MAIN advantage of an open heater is that it
    A. can separate scale forming substances from the feed-water by precipitation
    B. produces hotter water
    C. can hold more steam
    D. is cheap to operate

11. How much steam supply is sufficient for an open heater?
    A. 3 to 5 lbs.   B. 5 to 7 lbs.   C. 8 to 10 lbs.   D. All of the above

12. _____ A(n)   should be installed on an open feedwater heater
    A. exhaust or vent pipe   B. oil separator
    C. steam gauge   D. all of the above

13. A closed feedwater heater is a heater in which
    A. steam travels through coils or tubes and water on the outside of the coils
    B. water runs through a tube with steam on the outside heating the water
    C. feedwater is heated and passed back to the deaerator
    D. none of the above

14. At what pressure should a feedwater heater operate?
    A. 1-15 lbs.   B. 15-20 lbs.   C. 20-25 lbs.   D. 25-30 lbs.

15. The safety device normally installed on a feedwater heater is a _____ valve.
    A. pneumatic   B. pressure relief
    C. safety   D. by-pass

16. The FIRST indication of a broken coil on a feedwater heater would be the
    A. heater filling up with water
    B. relief valve opening
    C. steam pressure increasing
    D. water pressure rising

17. On a double-acting reciprocating pump, what is installed on the discharge side of the pump? A(n)
    A. air chamber and gauge
    B. pressure gauge and relief valve.
    C. pressure gauge and safety valve
    D. air chamber and a gate valve

18. What types of lubricators are MOST commonly used today?
    I. Hydrokinetic   II. Force feed pump
    III. Splash system   IV. Gravity

    The CORRECT answer is:
    A. I, II   B. II, III, IV   C. I, III, IV   D. I, II, III, IV

19. What type of lubricant is used on piston rods and valve stems on a reciprocating pump? 19.____
Mineral oil
    A. Compress oil
    B. Oil with high velocity
    C. Cylinder oil and graphite mixed together
    D. A reciprocating pump contains the following notation:

20. What is the diameter of the liquid cylinder? 7 x 6 x 4. 20.____
    A. 6"   B. 4"
    C. 7"   D. none of the above

21. What types of pumps are used in a heating system? 21.____
    I. Reciprocating   II. Condensate
    III. Centrifugal   IV. Vacuum

    The CORRECT answer is:
    A. I, II   B. I, III
    C. II, IV   D. III, IV

22. The purpose of a steam loop, or thermal pump, is to 22.____
    A. deliver steam to the engine
    B. protect water from entering the steam gauge
    C. return condensate back to the boiler
    D. trap steam from high pressure lines into a low-pressure line

23. What effect does a short stroke have on a reciprocating pump? It 23.____
    A. increases the pump capacity
    B. increases the steam capacity, and decreases the pump consumption
    C. increases the steam Consumption, and decreases the pump capacity
    D. relieves the pressure in the air chamber

24. A pump with two liquid cylinders, and one steam cylinder is called a pump. 24.____
    A. triplex   B. duplex
    C. tandem   D. double tandem

25. The air chamber on a reciprocating pump is located on the 25.____
    A. discharge side of the feed pump
    B. discharge side of the reciprocating pump
    C. discharge side of all pumps
    D. suction side of a reciprocating pump

KEY (CORRECT ANSWERS)

1. A	11. D
2. B	12. D
3. D	13. A
4. B	14. A
5. D	15. B
6. C	16. B
7. D	17. B
8. D	18. D
9. C	19. D
10. C	20. A

21. C
22. C
23. B
24. C
25. B

EXAMINATION SECTION
TEST 1

DIRECTIONS: Each question or incomplete statement is followed by several suggested answers or completions. Select the one that BEST answers the question or completes the Statement. *PRINT THE LETTER OF THE CORRECT ANSWER IN THE SPACE AT THE RIGHT.*

1. What type of pump has a diffusion *ring*?

    A. Centrifugal
    B. Duplex double acting
    C. Helical gear
    D. Spur gear

    1.____

2. A cause of excessive oil consumption in an air compressor is

    A. oil with improper viscosity
    B. defective discharge valve
    C. oil level too high in oil sump
    D. loose unloader unit

    2.____

3. How does cylinder oil compare with engine oil at engine room temperature? Cylinder oil

    A. is lighter in color
    B. has a higher viscosity
    C. has a lower viscosity
    D. is lighter when put in front of a light

    3.____

4. On a boiler-feed centrifugal pump, to maintain a certain speed, 60 horsepower is used. To double that speed, so as to obtain double the output, how much horsepower is needed?

    A. 120   B. 240   C. 360   D. 480

    4.____

5. The *slip* of a pump refers to

    A. lost motion on the steam slide valve
    B. leakage past the plunger on an outside packed pump
    C. recirculation of liquid from discharge side back to suction side
    D. clearance when piston is slipped inside cylinder

    5.____

6. On a reciprocating vacuum pump, the diameter of the steam piston is _____ the liquid piston.

    A. larger than
    B. smaller than
    C. the same size as
    D. twice the diameter of

    6.____

7. How many valves are there on the water end of a duplex double-acting feed pump?

    A. 8   B. 6   C. 4   D. 2

    7.____

8. Which of the following would you find on a duplex pump?

   A. Springs and packing
   B. Gears and impeller
   C. Flywheel and crank
   D. Crankshaft and air chamber

9. The function of the air chamber on a duplex, double-acting pump is to

   A. prevent hammering
   B. increase capacity of pump
   C. aerate the water
   D. prevent cavitation

10. The valve discs on the water end of a duplex pump are USUALLY made of

    A. wood
    B. steel
    C. rubber
    D. cast iron

11. A direct-acting, duplex steam pump *short strokes* when it returns from overhaul. The PROBABLE cause is

    A. feed water too cold
    B. steam pressure too low
    C. steam valves not properly set
    D. water discharge pressure too high

12. A heavy duty pump is one which

    A. is designed for the pumping of heavy liquids
    B. pumps large quantities of water
    C. has a high thermal efficiency
    D. is made of extra heavy material for high head pressure

13. When a punch is used in making holes for rivets or boiler tubes, the diameter of the punch shall be _____ the desired hole.

    A. three-quarters of the diameter of
    B. slightly smaller than
    C. exactly the same size as
    D. slightly larger than

14. On a _____ pump, you would find a *volute*.

    A. reciprocating
    B. centrifugal
    C. jet
    D. direct-pressure

15. In starting a centrifugal boiler feed pump with 300 lbs. water pressure on the line, the valves should be set with suction _____ and discharge _____.

    A. open; open
    B. open; closed
    C. closed; closed
    D. closed; open

16. On a centrifugal boiler feed pump, the regulating valve functions to maintain

    A. speed constant
    B. pressure constant
    C. variable speed
    D. water level

17. With centrifugal pumps, the head varies directly as the 17.____

    A. speed
    B. speed squared
    C. speed cubed
    D. diameter squared

18. An intercooler is used on a 18.____

    A. compound engine
    B. two-stage air compressor
    C. two-stage turbine
    D. two-stage evactor

19. The unloader on an air compressor is provided for 19.____

    A. reducing pressure
    B. easy starting
    C. high-starting pressure
    D. reducing temperature

20. A duplex center outside a packed feed water pump has 20.____

    A. yoke rod
    B. two water plungers
    C. compound steam glands
    D. four water pistons

21. A centrifugal pump operates with a high suction lift, which would require _____ line. 21.____

    A. lift check at bottom of suction
    B. swing check in discharge
    C. stop valve in discharge
    D. lift check at top of suction

22. Diffuser vanes will MOST generally be found in a _____ pump. 22.____

    A. centrifugal turbine
    B. centrifugal volute
    C. rotary
    D. reciprocating

23. A sewer ejector would be located 23.____

    A. on the roof of a building
    B. in the basement
    C. in the sub-basement
    D. in the sewer

24. How many pots are there on a double-acting water pump? 24.____

    A. 1   B. 2   C. 3   D. 4

25. What is the amount of steam consumption of a simple, duplex steam pump, in lbs./H.P. hour? 25.____

    A. 5-20   B. 25-35   C. 50-90   D. 120-200

KEY (CORRECT ANSWERS)

1. A
2. C
3. B
4. D
5. B

6. B
7. A
8. A
9. A
10. C

11. C
12. D
13. D
14. B
15. A

16. D
17. B
18. B
19. A
20. B

21. A
22. A
23. C
24. D
25. A

TEST 2

DIRECTIONS: Each question or incomplete statement is followed by several suggested answers or completions. Select the one that BEST answers the question or completes the statement. *PRINT THE LETTER OF THE CORRECT ANSWER IN THE SPACE AT THE RIGHT.*

1. The type of valve on a duplex steam pump is   1.____

    A. sleeve
    B. piston
    C. D-slide valve
    D. poppet

2. The slide valve on a Knowles pump is operated by   2.____

    A. linkage attached to the piston rod
    B. rocker arm of opposite steam slide
    C. an auxiliary piston
    D. discharge water pressure

3. A duplex, double-acting pump with the valves properly adjusted will   3.____

    A. not start sometimes
    B. always start
    C. jig
    D. start when off dead center

4. If one valve stem of a duplex, double-acting pump broke, the pump would   4.____

    A. increase in speed
    B. run slower
    C. stop
    D. run on one side only

5. The diameter of the steam cylinders of an 18 x 16 x 24 duplex, direct-acting steam pump is _____ inches.   5.____

    A. 18   B. 16   C. 24   D. 30

6. On a boiler feed pump, the   6.____

    A. steam cylinder is always larger than the water cylinder
    B. water cylinder is always larger than the steam cylinder
    C. cylinders are of equal size
    D. water discharge pipe is always larger than the suction pipe

7. Flax packing is used for   7.____

    A. steam end of pump
    B. water end of pump
    C. between flanges of pipe lines
    D. high temperature

8. Water is dripping out of the gland of a centrifugal pump used to pump feed water. You should   8.____

    A. renew the packing at the first opportunity
    B. pull up the gland as tight as possible with an ordinary 6 inch pipe wrench

65

C. pull up the gland just to the point where water does not leak out
D. do nothing

9. On the initial tightening of a jam-type gland on a boiler-feed water pump to stop excessive leakage, you would pull up alternately on the hexagonal nuts _____ turn.

   A. 1/6 B. 1/2 C. 3/4 D. 1 full

10. Diffuser vanes will MOST generally be found in a _____ pump.

    A. centrifugal turbine
    B. centrifugal volute
    C. rotary
    D. reciprocating

11. If the consumption of lubricating oil in an air compressor is excessive, it is MOST likely due to

    A. using too high viscosity oil
    B. a defective discharge valve
    C. a loose unloader unit
    D. oil too high in sump

12. Which of the following statements is CORRECT about a Worthington steam-driven duplex double-acting boiler feed pump?

    A. Will always start in position in which it was stopped
    B. Will not start if stopped with one piston at extreme head end and other at dead center
    C. Speed is controlled by inertia type governor
    D. Dust of f must always be 25%

13. Centrifugal boiler feed pumps for large boilers with fluctuating loads are usually fitted with a system for recirculating or recycling.
    This is done to prevent

    A. excessive head pressure
    B. loss of suction
    C. excessing governor action
    D. overheating with consequent flashing and seizing of the pump

14. In the operation of a turbo-driven centrifugal pump, the delivery of the pump would PROPERLY be controlled by

    A. throttling the discharge
    B. throttling the suction
    C. using a bypass
    D. throttling the steam supply

15. Assume that it is necessary to pump 40 M.G.D. against a 65 ft. head.
    If the pump efficiency is 65%, the B.H.P. of this pump is MOST NEARLY

    A. 920 B. 700 C. 460 D. 176

16. Assume that a pump had to be shut down temporarily due to trouble which was first reported by an oiler.
    The one of the following entries in the log concerning this occurrence which is LEAST important is

    A. time of the shutdown
    B. period of time the pump was out of service
    C. cause of the trouble
    D. time the oiler came on shift

17. At sea level, the theoretical maximum distance, in feet, the water can be lifted by suction *only* is MOST NEARLY

    A. 12.00   B. 14.70   C. 33.57   D. 72.00

18. While a lubricating oil is in use, for good performance, its neutralization number should

    A. keep rising
    B. remain about the same
    C. be greater than 0.1
    D. be greater than 2.0

19. The parts of a large sewage pump that would MOST likely need repairs after the fewest number of hours of operation are the

    A. pump casings
    B. impellers
    C. wearing rings
    D. outboard bearings

20. Flexible coupling used to connect a pump to an electric motor valve is USUALLY rated in horsepower per

    A. 100 rpm of shaft
    B. 300 rpm of shaft
    C. square inch of shaft area
    D. inch of shaft diameter

KEY (CORRECT ANSWERS)

1.	C	11.	D
2.	B	12.	A
3.	B	13.	D
4.	C	14.	D
5.	A	15.	B
6.	A	16.	D
7.	B	17.	C
8.	D	18.	B
9.	A	19.	C
10.	A	20.	A

BASIC FUNDAMENTALS OF WATER QUALITY

TABLE OF CONTENTS

	Page
Reasons for Water Treatment	1
Quality Control Tests	2
Drinking Water Standards	3
Composition of Water from Various Sources	5
Self-Purification and Storage	8
Methods of Water Treatment	10

BASIC FUNDAMENTALS OF WATER QUALITY

Water, if strictly defined in the chemical sense, is H_2O a compound which, like all other pure substances, has a definite and constant composition. Therefore it should, like any pure compound, exhibit predictable chemical and physical characteristics. Indeed, the properties of a pure compound are so dependable that they may be used for identification if an unknown sample is submitted to a laboratory. In other words, water might be expected to be the same, regardless of its origin. In this context, discussing the "quality" of water, or of water from a particular source, would be rather meaningless.

One of the predictable physical properties of this widely distributed compound is a rather remarkable power to dissovle other materials. Familiar as we are with its characteristics, we tend to accept the solvent power of water as a matter of course, and to see nothing remarkable in it. But if water is compared with other known liquids, it is found that none of the others is capable of dissolving so wide a range of compounds of varying compositions. As a result, water seldom if very occurs in nature in a chemically pure state.

In addition to a variety of dissolved materials, water drawn from a natural source usually contains particles of insoluble, or at least undissolved, materials in suspension. The size and the concentration of these suspended particles vary considerably, depending upon the source, from the sand grains sometimes present in rapid, turbulent surface streams to the submicroscopic dispersions known as colloids. Included among the suspended particles, there may be living cells of thousands of different kinds of microorganisms.

Thus, when we speak of the quality of water, our concern is not really with the water itself, but with the other materials present. It is these impurities which determine, to a very large degree, the suitability of a water source for human uses, the problems associated with utilizing it, and the kind and extent of treatment required.

Reasons for Water Treatment

In the broadest possible terms, the objectives of water treatment may be classified under three general headings: (1) to protect the health of the community, (2) to supply a product which is esthetically desirable, and (3) to protect the property of the consumers. Each of these is so broad that it requires further explanation, and each embraces several specific methods of treatment.

Protection of the public health implies first that the treated water must be free of microorganisms capable of causing human disease, and second that the concentrations of any chemical substances which are poisonous or otherwise harmful must be reduced to safe levels. Only rarely do raw water supplies contain significant levels of toxic chemicals. But, more often than not, the microbiological quality of the water requires improvement or protection. In the United States, this aspect of water treatment has progressed to the point that the physiological safety of public water supplies usually is taken for granted. In some parts of the world, it is considered necessary when visiting a strange city to carry a private supply of drinking water, or to inquire whether it is safe to drink the local supply. The situation in the United States, which is unquestionably a credit to the water treatment profession, has permitted increased attention to the other two general objectives mentioned in the previous paragraph.

An esthetically desirable water supply requires that the final product shall be as low as possible in color, turbidity, and suspended solids, as cold as possible, and free from undesirable tastes and odors. Since the subject of tastes and odors is highly subjective, it may be impossible to produce a product which is equally pleasing to all consumers. However, strong, distinctive tastes and odors, as well as those which are disagreeable to a significant percentage of the population, are definitely to be avoided. The esthetic quality of a water supply cannot be completely divorced from the question of public health, since objections to the taste, odor, color, etc. of a perfectly safe public supply may prompt consumers to use water from another source which is more attractive, but which, due to lack of protection, may be considerably more dangerous.

The question of property protection is a broad one, and its specific implications depend upon the purpose for which the water is used. Thus the requirements may, and occasionally do, vary among different consumers using the same supply. For domestic supplies, the usual requirements are that the water shall not be excessively corrosive to plumbing and other metal equipment, that it shall not deposit troublesome quantities of scale, and that it shall not stain porcelain plumbing fixtures. For industrial purposes, the requirements may be even more stringent. For example, more than 10 ppm of chlorides interfere with the manufacture of insulating paper. Generally speaking, public suppliers do not find it practical to meet the strict and sometimes varied requirements of their industrial customers. Instead, they maintain a quality suitable for domestic consumption, and if necessary the industries provide further treatment on their own premises.

Quality Control Tests

In his efforts to maintain the quality of his product, the operator or superintendent of a water treatment plant relies upon various chemical and physical tests. In this way, he accomplishes several purposes. Most importantly, perhaps, he assures himself of his success in meeting the standards which are required and desired. If for any reason the quality temporarily becomes unsatisfactory, the test results advise him of the problem, and permit prompt corrective action. By keeping permanent records of the results, he is in a position to demonstrate the quality of his product to the regulatory authorities, or to any other interested individual or agency.

Tests used for monitoring or controlling water quality are suggested by the objectives listed in the previous section. Few, if any, plants find it necessary to perform all the tests discussed in this manual. Ordinarily, the only tests selected for frequent, regular performance are those pertinent to the quality problems experienced at a particular plant. Other tests may be run less frequently to periodically provide a more complete evaluation of the water quality. Samples of the raw water as well as the treated water are often analyzed, since the former may provide information which is necessary to the control of the treatment plant. In some types of treatment, it is desirable in addition to analyze samples collected at intermediate points. Many suppliers also find it advisable to test samples collected from various parts of the distribution system to assure that the water quality is as acceptable when it reaches the consumer as when it leaves the treatment plant.

Determinations of bacteriological quality are most often based upon measurements of the numbers of "coliform bacteria." Although this group of organisms is not known to cause human disease directly, its presence and survival is considered to indicate the potential presence of disease organisms (pathogens), and consequently the number of coliforms present is strictly regulated. In some plants, the enumeration of coliforms is supplemented by the "total plate count," which is an approximate measurement of the total microbial population of the water, or by determining the numbers of one particular species of the coliform group, *Escherichia coli*.

In the vast majority of plants, especially in the United States, control of the bacteriological quality of the water is accomplished by means of chlorination. Therefore, the determination of residual chlorine in its various forms becomes a most important analysis, even though it may not be rigorously correct to consider it a direct means of monitoring the water quality. Closely related to the measurement of residual chlorine is the determination of chlorine demand, which is currently defined as the difference between the concentration of chlorine added and the concentration remaining after a specified period of time. Measurement of the chlorine demand of the raw water is often essential to successful control of the bacteriological quality of the finished product, particularly if the chlorine demand of the source tends to be variable.

Tests for chemical substances known to be poisonous are not ordinarily conducted routinely unless there is reason to suspect the presence of one or more such materials. If the previous history of the water supply, or other circumstance, indicates the possibility of a problem of this kind, the analytical program should include measurement of the concentration of the offending substance, probably both before and after treatment. Otherwise, tests of this type might be included among those which are performed only periodically.

Among the tests related to the esthetic quality of the water, determinations of color, turbidity, suspended solids, and temperature are important. The measurement of taste and odor, unfortunately, is almost as subjective in the laboratory as in the consumer's home or place of business, notwithstanding various attempts to improve its quantitative aspects. For this reason, some plants, in which taste and odor problems are rare, seldom if ever perform the determinations routinely, but rely upon complaints to advise them of the occurrence of a problem. In other places, less fortunate, where strong or disagreeable tastes and odors are a frequent problem, such tests may be a regular part of the quality control program. In a few instances, specific substances such as sulfides and phenols, which are known to affect taste and odor may be measured. Likewise, the determination of iron and manganese may be included in this group, because excessive quantities of either may affect both taste and color. The measurement of dissolved oxygen is sometimes included too, since the majority of people seem to prefer the flavor of water in which the oxygen content is near saturation.

For domestic purposes, the analyses related to protection of property include those which reveal the tendency of the water to corrode metals or to deposit scale. The important tests in this group are those for pH, acidity, alkalinity, total hardness, and calcium. Sometimes a determination of conductivity and total solids may be included, and under certain circumstances a measurement of the concentration of sulfates is important.

Drinking Water Standards

The U. S. Department of Health, Education, and Welfare, through its agency, the U. S. Public Health Service, has published revised standards for the quality of drinking water. Although the federal Public Health Regulations govern only interstate carriers and certain other specified installations, their standards are widely used as guide by other regulatory agencies. Many of the latter have incorporated the PHS standards wholly or in part into their own rules.

Some of the provisions of the Public Health Service standards are summarized below. It must be noted, however, that the complete report[1] from which this information is abstracted includes a great deal of supplementary material which is important in the interpretation and application of the standards. Therefore, the figures quoted do not apply strictly nor without qualification in all cases.

The standard of bacteriological quality is based upon the number of coliform bacteria present. Detailed sampling and testing procedures are specified, and a complete and fairly elaborate description of the method of evaluation sets forth precisely what results are required of an acceptable supply. In effect, the number of coliform bacteria is limited to not more than one organism per 100 ml of water on the average, with not more than five per cent of the samples tested showing numbers greater than this limit.

In regard to physical properties, the turbidity should be less than five units, the color less than 15 units, and the threshold odor number less than three. If the turbidity standard is satisfied, the suspended solids will not be detectable.

"Recommended" limits of concentration established for a number of chemical substances appear in Table VII. These are not absolute standards. Rather it is suggested that these materials "should not be present in a water supply in excess of the listed concentrations where . . . other more suitable supplies are or can be made available."

TABLE I
RECOMMENDED CONCENTRATION LIMITS

Substance	Maximum Concentration, mg/l
Alkyl Benzene Sulfonate	0.5
Arsenic	0.01
Chloride	250.
Copper	1.
Carbon Chloroform Extract	0.2
Cyanide	0.01
Fluoride	0.8-1.7 (See PHS Standards)
Iron	0.3
Manganese	0.05
Nitrate	45.
Phenols	0.001
Sulfate	250.
Total Dissolved Solids	500.
Zinc	5.

In addition to the recommended standards which appear in Table I, concentration limits for certain constituents are established which may be considered absolute, in that exceeding any one of the limits listed provides grounds for rejecting the supply. These figures appear in Table II.

TABLE II
ABSOLUTE CONCENTRATION LIMITS

Substance	Maximum Concentration, mg/l
Arsenic	0.05
Barium	1.0
Cadmium	0.01
Chromium, Hexavalent	0.05
Cyanide	0.2
Fluoride	See Text
Lead	0.05
Selenium	0.01
Silver	0.05

For Fluoride, both the recommended and absolute limits are related to the climate of the locality in question. For the greatest part of New York State, the recommended optimum is 1.1 mg/l, the recommended upper limit is 1.5 mg/l and the absolute limit is 2.2 mg/l. For a small area in the northern part of the state, the corresponding limits are 1.2, 1.7 and 2.4 mg/l, and in the extreme southeastern part, 1.0, 1.3 and 2.0 mg/l.

Radioactivity is also limited, but the acceptability of a given supply is dependent to some extent upon exposure from other sources. A water supply is unconditionally acceptable in this respect if the content of Radium 226 is less than three micro-micro-curies per liter, the content of Strontium 90 is less than 10 micro-micro-curies per liter, and the gross beta-ray activity is less than one microcurie per liter. If the radioactivity of the water supply exceeds the values stated, then its acceptability is judged on the basis of consideration of other sources of radioactivity in the environment.

Composition of Water from Various Sources

As suggested before, virtually all the water used to supply human requirements has at some time, usually quite recently, fallen to the surface of the earth as rain or some other form of precipitation. At this stage, the quantity of foreign material it contains is likely to be at a minimum. Nevertheless, even rain water is not chemically pure H_2O. Not only does it dissolve the gases of the atmosphere as it falls, but it also collects dust and other solid materials suspended in the air. Since the atmospheric solids depend upon both the composition of the soil below and the materials released into the air from combustion, industrial processes, and other sources, analyses of rain or other forms of precipitation reveal surprising variations. In general, however, rainwater may be expected to be very soft, to be low in total solids and alkalinity, to have a pH value somewhat below neutrality, and to be quite corrosive to many metals. A "typical" analysis, subject to the variations mentioned above, might appear as follows:

Hardness	19	mg/l as $CaCO_3$
Calcium	16	mg/l as $CaCO_3$
Magnesium	3	mg/l as $CaCO_3$
Sodium	6	mg/l as Na
Ammonium	0.8	mg/l as N
Bicarbonate	12	mg/l as $CaCO_3$
Acidity	4	mg/l as $CaCO_3$
Chloride	9	mg/l as Cl
Sulfate	10	mg/l as SO_4
Nitrate	0.1	mg/l as N
pH	6.8	

After the water reaches the surface of the ground, it passes over soil and rock into lakes, streams, and reservoirs, or it percolates through the soil and rock into the ground water. In the process, a great variety of materials may be dissolved or taken into suspension. Consequently, it may be expected that the composition of both the surface waters and the ground water of a given area reflects the geology of the region, that is, the composition of the underlying rock formations and of the soils derived from them. In general, the presence of readily soluble formations near the surface, such as gypsum, rock salt, or the various forms of limestone, produce relatively marked effects upon the waters of the area. On the other hand, in the presence of less soluble formations, such as sandstone or granite, the composition of the water tends to remain more like that of rain. As one might expect, local variations are often considerable and occasionally extreme, both in the concentration of any one constituent and in the proportions of the various materials present. The examples given below should be considered with this in view. They are typical only in that they are not remarkable.

Surface water, in an area in which limestone is an important constituent of the geologic formations, might have a composition similar to the following:

Hardness	120	mg/l as $CaCO_3$
Calcium	80	mg/l as $CaCO_3$
Magnesium	40	mg/l as $CaCO_3$
Sodium & Potassium	19	mg/l as Na
Bicarbonate	106	mg/l as $CaCO_3$
Chloride	23	mg/l as Cl
Sulfate	38	mg/l as SO_4
Nitrate	0.4	mg/l as N
Iron	0.3	mg/l as Fe
Silica	18	mg/l as SiO_2
Carbon Dioxide	4	mg/l as $CaCO_3$
pH	7.8	

In such an area, the ground water often contains more hardness and bicarbonate than the surface waters. This is due in part to the longer period of contact with soil and rock, and in part to the fact that carbon dioxide, contributed by the decomposition of organic matter in the soil, greatly increases the solubility of some of the constituents. The folowing analysis might be considered typical of well or spring water in a limestone area:

Hardness	201	mg/l as $CaCO_3$
Calcium	142	mg/l as $CaCO_3$
Magnesium	59	mg/l as $CaCO_3$
Sodium & Potassium	20	mg/l as Na
Bicarbonate	143	mg/l as $CaCO_3$
Chloride	23	mg/l as Cl
Sulfate	59	mg/l as SO_4
Nitrate	0.06	mg/l as N
Iron	0.18	mg/l as Fe
Silica	12	mg/l as SiO_2
Carbon Dioxide	14	mg/l as $CaCO_3$
pH	7.4	

In areas in which the underlying formations are insoluble, that is, where they consist of sand, sandstone, clay, shale, or igneous rocks, the waters tend to he softer and more acid. In general, their content of most dissolved materials is lower. Acidity, however, may be higher than in hard water areas, since carbon dioxide picked up from the soil is not neutralized. Excepting in some areas of igneous rock, iron also tends to be higher in soft waters, since many of the iron compounds of soils and rocks are dissolved by the acidity of the waters. In many soft water areas, the differences between ground waters and surface waters are not as pronounced as in hard water regions, although many exceptions to this generality could be cited.

A more or less typical analysis of surface water in a region of generally insoluble soils and rocks follows:

Hardness	46	mg/l as $CaCO_3$
Calcium	30	mg/l as $CaCO_3$
Magnesium	16	mg/l as $CaCO_3$
Sodium & Potassium	9	mg/l as Na
Bicarbonate	42	mg/l as $CaCO_3$
Chloride	5	mg/l as Cl
Sulfate	12	mg/l as SO_4

Nitrate	1.5	mg/l as N
Iron	1.1	mg/l as Fe
Silica	30	mg/l as SiO_2

Ground water from a similar region might give analytical results similar to the following:

Hardness	61	mg/l as $CaCO_3$
Calcium	29	mg/l as $CaCO_3$
Magnesium	32	mg/l as $CaCO_3$
Sodium	26	mg/l as Na
Bicarbonate	60	mg/l as $CaCO_3$
Chloride	7	mg/l as Cl
Sulfate	17	mg/l as SO_4
Carbon Dioxide	59	mg/l as $CaCO_3$
PH	6.6	
Iron	1.8	mg/l as Fe

It is worth re-emphasizing that each of the constituents listed in the analyses above may vary over a wide range from place to place.

For example, waters are known with hardness values of less than 10 mg/l, and others have concentrations over 1,000 mg/l. Those quoted have been chosen to represent rather moderate, ordinary values occurring in two distinct types of situations common in the United States. It would be a mistake, however, to expect any water sample to correspond exactly to any one of the analyses given as examples.

Good Quality Water. Since waters from various sources may vary so markedly in composition, one may reasonably question which source should be considered most desirable. The problem has several practical consequences. For example, if a choice exists among several available sources, the final decision may rest upon judgment of their relative quality. Also, when the composition is modified by treatment, the objective is to approach, if not always to attain, the ideal.

The characteristics of "good quality water" are implied in earlier sections of this chapter, which discuss the objectives of water treatment and the standards formally adopted by the U.S. Public Health Service. Reviewing those sections will make it evident that the properties desired are mostly negative. That is, the objectives and standards are directed principally to avoiding undesirable qualities. The properties of " good" water may then be summarized in qualitative terms as follows:

1. Absence of harmful concentrations of poisonous chemical substances
2. Absence of the causative microorganisms and viruses of disease
3. Lowest possible levels of color, turbidity, suspended solids, odor, and taste
4. Lowest possible temperature
5. Minimum corrosivity to metals
6. Least possible tendency to deposit scale
7. Lowest possible content of staining materials, such as iron, manganese, and copper

This may appear to suggest that the ideal water contains the lowest possible quantity of total solids but this is not the case. Extremely soft waters tend to be excessively corrosive to metals, and many persons find them unpalatable. Moreover, they seem to be less effective in removing soap by rinsing than waters containing a little hardness.

Although there has been no formal recognition of a set of analytical values characterizing the "ideal" water, the following would probably be considered generally acceptable as an approximation:

Alkyl Benzene Sulfonate	less than 0.1 mg/l, preferably 0
Arsenic	less than 0.01 mg/l, preferably 0
Barium	less than 1 mg/l, preferably 0
Bicarbonate*	150 mg/l as $CaCO_3$
Cadium	less than 0.01 mg/l, preferably 0
Calcium*	70 mg/l as $CaCO_3$
Carbon Chloroform Extract	less than 0.2 mg/l, preferably 0
Carbon Dioxide*	6 mg/1 as $CaCO_3$
Chloride*	less than 250 mg/l, preferably 0
Chromium, Hexavalent	less than 0.05 mg/l, preferably 0
Coliform Bacteria	less than 1 per 100 ml
Color	less than 15 units, preferably 0
Copper	less than 1 mg/l, preferably 0
Cyanide	less than 0.01 mg/l, preferably 0
Fluoride	approximately 0.9 mg/l (somewhat dependent upon climate)
Hardness*	70 mg/l as $CaCO_3$
Iron	less than 0.1 mg/l, preferably 0
Lead	less than 0.05 mg/l, preferably 0
Magnesium*	preferably 0
Manganese	less than 0.02 mg/l, preferably 0
Nitrate	less than 10 mg/l, preferably 0
pH*	7.8
Phenols	less than 0.001 mg/l, preferably 0
Selenium	less than 0.01 mg/l, preferably 0
Silver	less than 0.05 mg/l, preferably 0
Sodium & Potassium*	37 mg/l as Na
Sulfate*	less than 250 mg/l, preferably 0
Suspended Solids	not detectable
Temperature	33 to 40 degrees Fahrenheit
Threshold Odor Number	less than 3, preferably 0
Total Dissolved Solids	less than 500 mg/l
Turbidity	less than 5 units, preferably 0
Zinc	less than 5 mg/l, preferably 0

*The relationships among calcium, bicarbonate, carbon dioxide, and pH should be such as to minimize scaling and corrosion. In some cases, these concentrations may dictate the most desirable concentrations of sulfate, chloride, magnesium, sodium, and potassium.

Self-Purification and Storage

Nature provides some degree of self-purification for all water that has been polluted or contaminated by the introduction of wastes, whether they originate as domestic sewage, industrial wastes, or drainage from yards, streets, and agricultural areas. The rate at which process occurs depends upon the nature and amount of polluting material as well as the physical, chemical, and biological conditions and characteristics of the water itself. Erroneous ideas are prevalent, however, particularly as to the value of aeration and its effect on flowing water. For instance, statements are sometimes made to the effect that "water will purify itself in flowing seven miles," or that natural aeration occurring at waterfalls and rapids will "oxidize" or kill bacteria. Actually, distance in itself has nothing whatever to do with self-purification in a flowing stream. Neither does aeration have much if any direct effect in killing bacteria. Time is the important factor, together wth proper conditions of temperature, sunlight, velocity of flow and many other complex chemical, physical, and biological characteristics. Quiescent sedimentation in a reservoir for a period of about a month may result generally in purification equivalent to that of filtration. Sluggish flow in a stream for a long distance may accomplish the same results.

The general appearance of a stream provides a useful guide to the degree of pollution. For instance, the bed of the unpolluted portion above sources of wastewaters usually is coated with a greenish brown deposit and green, rooted plants will thrive in protected areas. Just below a point of pollution, chemical and biological changes are evident, such as the gradual disappearance of the green plants. This stretch of the stream has been called the "zone of recent pollution."

Further downstream is the "zone of active decomposition", where the bed of the stream may have black sludge deposits, and a characteristic biological population adapted to a plentiful food supply but a limited oxygen supply. If the degree of pollution is great, the dissolved oxygen of the water may be completely exhausted. This results generally in objectionable conditions, the production of odors and gases, and a turbid gray or black appearance of the water. If, on the other hand, the degree of pollution is moderate and the dissolved oxygen content of the water is sufficient, odors are not produced. This condition results when the dissolved oxygen is replenished from the atmosphere and plant life at a rate faster than it is being used up in oxidation of the polluting material. The presence of rapids, falls, or even swiftly flowing water in this zone is helpful insofar as providing an adequate supply of atmospheric oxygen is concerned, since the rate of reaeration is closely related to the turbulence of the water. It should be noted, however, that a supply of oxygen exceeding the requirements does not accelerate the natural purification processes. Since the time is not shortened, a high flow velocity only means that the distance traveled before purification is complete is increased.

Eventually, unless additional pollution is discharged into the stream, the result is the production of an odorless, humus-like material in the stream bed. If the pollution contained nitrogenous materials, the concentration of nitrates in the water increases. There is restoration of the normal dissolved oxygen content, which favors the growth of green aquatic vegetation. Normal conditions are thus restored in this "zone of recovery," the length and position of which are dependent upon the degree of pollution and the natural conditions outlined above.

Essentially, the same action takes place in a natural lake or in an impounding reservoir, although the "zones" described above may not exist as distinct regions. This is due to the complications which are caused by the lack of currents with definite direction. Furthermore, a considerable amount of vertical mixing may occur due to variations in the density of the water. The changes of density, in turn, are caused by the differences of temperature of the water at the various levels in the lake or reservoir. The vertical mixing takes place continuously, but is most noticeable in the spring and fall when temperature changes are most rapid and mixing consequently most vigorous throughout the entire depth of the water. Very often this "turnover" of a lake or reservoir results in the occurrence of tastes and odors in the water supply, which may be due to changes in the types and numbers of microorganisms present, or to changes in the chemical and physical quality of the water.

In general, self-purification results in the removal of organic matter and the degree depends upon the dilution, the effectiveness of reaeration, sedimentation, and most important, the time interval available for biochemical action. The destruction of bacteria introduced with sewage, however, is controlled by a different set of factors. The rate is controlled by the water temperature, available food supply, the germicidal effect of sunlight, sedimentation, and the consumption of the bacteria as food by protozoa. This action is usually slower than the destruction of organic matter. Hence, bacterial contamination may persist long after the visible evidence of pollution has disappeared. Therefore, the only possible way of determining the influence of storage or of passage along a stream upon the bacteriological quality of the water is to measure bacterial numbers in representative samples of water collected at appropriate points.

Unfortunately, the effects of storage and time are not all beneficial in relation to certain characteristics of water. The results of biochemical purification are, for example, conductive to the growth of algae and other forms of microscopic plant and animal life. Although these organisms may have little if any effect on the health of a community as a result of drinking the water, they are the most common cause of tastes and odors, and generally, additional treatment is needed when they are present.

Methods of Water Treatment

The methods employed in the treatment of water depend, to a large extent, on the purpose for which the supply is to be used and the quality of the water being treated. For domestic use, it is desirable to remove any materials, either in suspension or in solution, which are detrimental to the appearance and esthetic appeal of the water. It is absolutely necessary to remove or kill any detrimental microorganisms, and to remove harmful chemical substances. On the other hand, industrial requirements for water quality vary, depending upon the use. For example, for stream generation the control of scale formation is of paramount importance, while textile mills and paper mills demand freedom from iron and manganese.

In general, the many methods normally employed in water treatment practice usually have as their main objective the reduction of the total quantity of foreign substances in the water. Even when the treatment process involves the addition of certain materials, the end result is usually the removal of more material than has been added. There are cases, however, in which certain constituents are removed by substituting other substances, and in some circumstances the content of certain substances may be increased deliberately, in order to impart certain desirable characteristics to the water.

Sedimentation. Sedimentation is more or less effective in the removal of suspended matter, depending upon the size and the density of the particles to be removed, and the time available for the process. Large or heavy particles are removed in a relatively short time, while a much longer period is required for light or finely divided materials. Some of the very finest such as eroded clay may not be removed even by several days' sedimentation. If the concentration of such "non-settleable" particles is excessive, then sedimentation alone is not an adequate method of treatment, and other means must be employed.

Coagulation. This is the technique of treating the water with certain chemicals for the purpose of collecting non-settleable particles into larger or heavier aggregates which are more readily removed. The resulting clumps of solid material, termed "floc," are removed by sedimentation, filtration, or both.

Filtration. Filtration of the water through sand, anthracite, diatomite, and other fine-grained materials is also capable of removing particulate matter too light or too finely divided to be removed by sedimentation. Filters often follow sedimentation units, so that the larger quantity of relatively coarse material is removed by sedimentation, to avoid rapid clogging of the filters, which in turn remove the particles for which sedimentation is not effective. Fine screens or microstrainers are sometimes used prior to sand filtration.

Disinfection. This broad sense means destroying pathogenic organisms. In the practice of water treatment in the United States, it is usually accomplished by the application of chlorine or certain chlorine compounds. Although many other treatment processes mentioned also have some effect upon the microbial population of the water, disinfection is the only step which is intended specifically for control of the bacteriological quality.

Softening. The removal of the elements which contribute hardness to a water supply, primarily calcium and magnesium is called softening. Many water supplies do not require softening, and in some cases, even though the water is hard, softening is not practiced. When domestic supplies are softened, usually the *lime-soda process* or the *ion-exchange process* is used. In the first, chemicals are added to precipitate calcium as calcium carbonate, and if further softening is required, magnesium is precipitated as magnesium hydroxide. Usually, the process results in a reduction of the total quantity of dissolved solids in the water. In the ion-exchange process, calcium and magnesium salts are converted to sodium salts, and little change in the total dissolved solids results.

Aeration. This may be used for a variety of purposes. Since volatile substances are removed in the process to some extent, and these may include materials which affect the taste and odor of the water, aeration is sometimes employed in connection with taste and odor control. Excessive carbon dioxide can also be removed in this way, and the corrosive effect of some water can be reduced. The removal of carbon dioxide by aeration sometimes also reduces the dosages of chemicals required in subsequent treatment processes. Finally, by supplying dissolved oxygen, aeration is often helpful in the removal of iron.

Iron and manganese removal. Specific processes to remove iron and manganese are employed only in waters which contain sufficient concentrations of these substances to cause persistent problems. A number of different techniques exist, and the choice depends upon the concentration and the chemical nature of the iron and manganese present.

Taste and odor removal. Taste and odor are affected by many of the treatment processes which are employed primarily for other purposes, and therefore, like some other characteristics, do not require special processes for control unless rather unusual problems exist. Which one of the several available processes proves to be most successful depends upon the nature and the concentration of the offending substances. It has been mentioned that some odors are effectively removed by aeration. Others may require either adsorption or oxidation for efficient control.

Corrosion control. This is accomplished in some cases by the removal of excess carbon dioxide (e.g., by aeration). In other cases, alkalinity is added to the water in the form of an alkaline chemical such as sodium carbonate.

Fluoridation. The objective of this process is to attain a concentration of fluoride in the water which imparts to the population the maximum degree of resistance to tooth decay.